LINE DANCE ESSENTIALS

A MUST HAVE GUIDE TO LINE DANCING

PETER HEATH

Copyright © Peter Heath 2016

All rights reserved. No part of this publication may be reproduced, stored in a retrieval system, or transmitted in any form or by any means electronic, mechanical, photocopying, recording or otherwise, without the prior written permission of the authors.

First published in Australia by Peter Heath.

Cover design and typesetting by Green Hill Publishing

ISBN: 978-0-9954067-6-6
All rights reserved. Printed in Australia.

CONTENTS

INTRODUCTION	1
FOR THE DANCERS	5
Can you become a Line Dancer?	5
Health Benefits of Line Dancing	7
Where can you go to learn Line Dancing?	11
Line Dance Choreography Structure	13
Dancing Technique for Line Dancing	14
Music	16
Body Mechanics	20
What should I wear as a Dancer?	22
Line Dance Specific Terminology	24
Choosing a Class	27
Going to Socials	28
Describing Line Dance Choreography	29
Dance Sheets	29
Limitations of Line Dance Choreography	35
Choreography Terminology	35
Line Dancer Competencies	64
Advanced Line Dance Techniques	65

FOR THE COACH — 75
- Performance Line Dancing — 76
- Competition Line Dancing — 80

FOR THE INSTRUCTOR — 81
- Venues — 82
- Know your Dancers and Yourself — 86
- Selecting the Dance Choreography to Teach — 93
- Cueing the Dance — 97
- Reading a Dance Sheet while Teaching — 101
- Theoretical Competency and Training Models — 101
- Voice Production — 103
- Teaching Techniques — 105
- Class Structure — 124
- Music and Line Dance — 127
- Presentation — 130
- Sound Equipment — 143
- Research and Training — 146
- Keeping your Suppliers Happy — 148
- Advertising and Promotion — 149
- I Hate that Dance! — 150
- I Hate That Song! — 150
- Line Dance Instructor Competencies — 151
- Your First Class — 152

FOR THE CELEBRITY OR WORKSHOP INSTRUCTOR — 155
- Find Out your Customers Expectations and Experience — 155
- Gather your Material — 156
- Select your Material — 157
- Choose the Order of Presentation — 157
- Present the Material — 158
- Review the Material — 159
- Get Honest Feedback — 159

FOR THE LINE DANCE EVENT COORDINATOR — 161
- Socials — 161
- Workshops — 164
- Longest, Largest, Line Attempts — 165
- Competitions — 166

FOR THE EVENT DJ — 177
- Making a Programme of Social Dances — 177
- Other tasks for a DJ — 182

FOR THE LINE DANCE MANAGER — 185
- Employee Run Line Dance Activity's — 185
- Entrepreneur Run Line Dance Activities — 186

FOR THE DISTRIBUTORS — 189
- Step Sheet Content and Format — 189
- Corrections — 190
- Searching — 190
- Website costs — 190

FOR THE SHEET WRITERS — 193
- Dance File Format — 193
- Dance Description — 194
- Music Information — 194
- Song Count In — 195
- Version Number — 195
- Choreographer Contact Information — 195
- Beat Punctuation — 196
- Documenting the Timing — 197
- Create Dance Progress Reference Points — 197
- Documenting the Turning — 197
- Suggesting the Chunking — 198
- Interruptions — 198
- Don't Mix Clusters into Detail Descriptions — 199

Use the Correct Words in the Descriptions	199
Completely Describe the Moves	201
Proof Reading the Sheet	201
FOR THE CHOREOGRAPHERS	**203**
Collaboration	204
Choosing a Dance Name	204
Music	205
Choosing the Moves	207
Be Considerate of Dancer Comfort and Well Being	212
Set the Correct Level of Your Dance	215
Choreographer Competencies	215
What makes a good Dance?	216
OUTSTANDING ISSUES IN LINE DANCING	**217**
Plagiarism in Line Dancing	217
Legacy Line Dances	218
Getting It Right	218
WHERE TO FROM HERE?	**221**
ACKNOWLEDGEMENTS	**223**

INTRODUCTION

What is Line Dancing?

Essentially line dancing is a group of people doing the same choreography to the same music at the same time in the same place in the same direction. But line dancing is so much more than that. Line dancing has become the most shared and "participated in" dance form on the planet. From its roots in the USA it has spread throughout the world across Asia, Europe and all other parts of the globe.

Origins of Line Dancing

Traditionally, like square dancing, line dancing (often called "Boot Scootin'") has its visible roots in the country music arena, with the earliest known country music associated line dances "Walkin' Wazi" and "Cowboy Boogie" created in 1972. This is not its true origins however. There were many dances being done in the disco era of the 1970's and earlier that fit the definition of line dancing. Dances such as the "The Bus Stop" from 1976, "The Madison" from 1957, "The Nutbush" from 1973, "The San Francisco Stomp" from 1961 and "Skywalker" from 1977, to name a few. Of course many ethnic and aboriginal groups have their form of line dance going back thousands of years. So finding the origins of line dancing is not as easy as it might seem.

What is the appeal of Line Dancing?

First and foremost, you don't need a partner. Unlike most other forms of social dance, there are no partners or deliberate physical contact in line dancing. Of course this doesn't stop people modifying the dances for couples, but essentially it is a non-contact form of dance. This appeals to the people without partners, or more likely those with partners that, for whatever reason, refuse to dance.

Secondly, you do not have to be a trained dancer to participate. Anybody can achieve some form of line dance success, with routines even choreographed for wheelchair and armchair dancers.

Thirdly and potentially the most important, there are significant health benefits to line dancing. It has been proved to be important in preventing or reducing Heart Disease, Osteoporosis, Vertigo, Arthritis, Depression and Dementia.

One of the important benefits to line dancing is the social contact that it provides to people who might otherwise not mix with others on a regular basis. Line dancing can be adapted to include all ages and abilities making it very versatile.

So why write this book?

Line dancing has developed enormously since its birth, and has flourished as a folk dance form for many years. But till now, it lacked the structure and standardisation of terminology of other forms of popular social dance, such as ballroom dancing or square dancing. Till now, there has been no international standard of documentation or description of the line dance choreography. Nor was there any easy to find and understand resource material for teachers or choreographers of line dance. I intend to hopefully solve that problem with this book.

There are three obvious groups of people critical to the development and well-being of line dancing.

- There are the choreographers who choose the music and create the dances that we all get to enjoy.

- Then there are the line dance teachers, usually called "Instructors" who research the dance sheets and work out how to get their customers to achieve what the choreographer intended.
- Of course there are the dancers who perform the choreography in classes and at social events.

There are also other groups of people that are less recognised, but equally important to making this international line dance movement work. They are:

- The dance sheet writers who try to capture the choreography in a written form. These people often are not the choreographers, but someone they have contracted to produce the sheet that describes their dance.
- The distributors that provide the opportunity for the choreographers to share their creations, via the internet or magazines.
- The coaches that coordinate the teams of dancers and competitors in their presentation efforts.
- The DJs who coordinate the music at special events, workshops and socials.
- The event coordinators who put events together for the line dance community.
- The celebrity or guest instructors who entertain and share new material.

This book is intended to provide knowledge to all these groups of people, to enhance their professionalism and enjoyment of our wonderful past-time.

Why me?

I have spent most of my lifetime teaching dancing. I started teaching square dancing and round dancing in the 1980's including calling and cueing at national conventions in the USA and Australia. I trained briefly as a ballroom dance teacher. I started line dance teaching in the boom era of 1993. Since then I have visited and taught line dancing at classes around the world, including Australia, Asia, Europe, North and South America, Africa and the Pacific region.

I have run (and still run) the largest commercial line dance organisation in the world, with over one hundred instructors working for and with me, at some stage, for well over two decades. My wife and I have developed an apprenticeship system to train our instructors, based on the content captured in this book.

We have been using translated electronic dance sheets on tablets for well over four years. These sheets are only possible due to the standardisation of layout and terminology that we have adopted. We all use the same terminology, music, teaching techniques, sound equipment, level structure and dance programme, to ensure compatibility between classes.

Over the decades I have been teaching, I have had to translate all the choreography we have attempted into a common language to make our organisation work effectively. This way all the instructors are using the same language and, when their dancers come together at social events, they all speak and understand the same terminology. The contents of this book capture that experience.

We are not dance competitors, we are not celebrities. We are not even famous. We are excellent teachers and promoters of line dance first and foremost.

I know it works. I hope there will be something here to help everyone, no matter what level of experience they have achieved in line dancing. I do not expect people to adopt all of it, but if there is an element that works for you then why not use it? That is better than no system at all.

This book is not intended to be read from cover to cover in one session. Later sections will become more relevant as you develop your line dance skills. Just read what is important now and save the rest till later. Alternatively, you might want to find out what is involved in the next stage of the line dance food chain.

So let's get started.

FOR THE DANCERS

Can you become a Line Dancer?

Most people are capable of becoming a line dancer. However there are some life skills that are necessary for interpreting the instructions and choreography in a standard class situation.

Group Walking

Soon after a child is born they learn to walk. Each individual person develops their own personal gait. A gait is the comfortable step size and comfortable step tempo, based on their individual height, weight and strength, and is adjusted to accommodate the terrain being walked over. Later children learn to run, and they develop a second, faster gait.

Later on in life, most people learn to walk in groups. This involves adjusting their individual gait to keep up with the average gait of the group. This may involve slowing down, or speeding up, or adjusting the size of the step, to avoid tripping or interfering with nearby walkers.

The military have taken group walking to the extreme, when they developed marching. By standardising the step size and step tempo for all personnel, they allow maximum transfer of people from one place to another, because they can travel much closer together without tripping. They practice this with marching drills, to override the natural individual gaits of the soldiers with the standard ones.

Line dancing utilises group walking skills to a very large degree. If everyone does not take the same size step, or they travel in a different direction, or step at a different speed, it can cause chaos on the dance floor.

Pre-Learner Competencies

These are the things you need to know, or be able to do, without assistance, before you can try to learn to line dance.

- Can Count to 8 and demonstrate an understanding of numbers
- Can understand fractional turning (half, quarter etc.), or can understand the analogue time concept of (3:00, 7:30 etc.) to demonstrate facing other directions on the dance floor.
- Can demonstrate knowledge of Left and Right, and demonstrate which is which (most of the time)
- Can physically move forward, back and sideways without turning the head and body
- Can demonstrate where the front of the dance floor is after turning multiple times.
- Can demonstrate an understanding of instructions given either visually or audibly.
- Can demonstrate group walking ability.
- Can retain knowledge and concentration for at least fifteen minutes.
- Has a positive attitude towards learning something new. Saying "I can't dance" is defeatist. Instead say, "I want to learn to dance."

People with disabilities

People with disabilities can learn to line dance provided they can still accomplish the above competencies. Hearing impaired people can "feel" the beat of most music, provided there is sufficient bass beat, so they can step in time to the music. Visually impaired people can use the music source as an audible reference to determine the front of the floor, and therefore other directions. Significantly movement impaired dancers can be very agile using their mobility devices, but will need a larger (sometimes much larger) personal space. People with lesser mobility issues can just take smaller steps in many situations.

Don't give up trying, it's worth it. If you have issues, please make the instructor aware of them so they can compensate with their teaching techniques. The only way to fail at line dancing is to stop coming to class.

People with Vertigo

Dizziness can instantly turn any dance from fun to terrifying. This dizziness is called vertigo. It is a sensation you get when you've spun too many times and the world is racing to catch up. Basically your brain gets confused as to where your body actually is in space, causing various stress-related reactions in the body. It can range from mild discomfort to complete disorientation and nausea.

People with vertigo or balance problems can be accommodated in line dancing by getting taught alternatives to any large turns to allow them to still execute most of the choreography. They can also be taught a technique called spotting that will reduce the impact of the turns.

This seems to be one of the major issues in line dancing with the senior customers.

Health Benefits of Line Dancing

The full benefits of line dancing may never fully be documented. Only in recent years are health studies being done to measure the effects of dancing on well-being. There are some very obvious effects that those of us that have been teaching for a long time have noticed.

Dementia and Alzheimer's – Because line dancers are constantly learning new routines and experiencing new steps and music, they are keeping their brains very active. Even trying to recall old dances keeps the brain ticking over. This, in my observation, reduces the likelihood of developing

Dementia. I know for a fact that, in our classes over the last two decades, we have lost way fewer people to these diseases than we should have, based on population statistics.

Osteoporosis – Line dancing constantly changes direction and turns frequently. There are lots of sideways and backwards movements rather than just forward movement. These movements cause both the muscles, and the bones, to strengthen in all directions, in quite a good "low impact" way. That is an improvement on exercise that is repetitive in one direction only, like walking for example. Line dancing can reduce the likelihood of muscle and bone wastage which could otherwise lead to Osteoporosis.

Heart Disease and Obesity Issues – Any exercise is good for your body. Line dancing is "sneaky" exercise. You concentrate on the steps, music and class interactions so much that you don't realise you have been exercising. Many young "fit" people, that line dance for the first time, are surprised how hard it is to keep up with the seniors that have been dancing regularly for years.

Arthritis – Keeping the bones moving will reduce the intensity of arthritis. Low impact, gentle exercise will keep the joints lubricated and less prone to seizing up.

Depression – Line dancing has the wonderful ability to remove all other thoughts from the mind while concentrating on the dance. Often a line dance class is the one place people can go to remove themselves from reality for a couple of hours. The social side of the dance class is also good therapy for the lonely or unhappy person.

Vertigo – It has been suggested in some studies that accustoming people to spinning in a dance class over a long period of time, might help uncouple the vestibular-ocular reflex from their perception of turning, and help them feel less vertigo.

Breaking Hips – The many sideways movements done in line dancing strengthen the muscles at the side of the hip, helping protect the hip from dislocation and other hip issues often experienced by the seniors in the community.

Generally it is just good exercise for the mind as well as the body.

The social aspect of line dancing is equally important as the health benefits. The routine of coming to class and befriending classmates may be the only outside social contact some people have. Running social activities outside of the regular class timeslot is also important in keeping the classmates happy and committed.

Note that doing two classes a week will give more than twice the benefit to your learning. That is because the time between classes is shorter, so you will retain more information from class to class. You will also get additional health benefits from more frequent exercise. A ninety minute class is equivalent to 4500 to 6000 steps as counted on a Fitbit.

Medical Studies of Benefits of Dancing

There was a recent German study comparing the benefits of a gym workout verses dancing.

"The results were unequivocal. Dancing wins every time. Why? It improves aerobic capacity, balance and spatial awareness. The need to remember steps exercises vital parts of the brain. If there is one message to come out of this programme, it is that we should all be cancelling our gym membership and hitting the dance class instead." Quote from BBC1 - 2016 - How to Stay Young

A 21 year study of senior citizens, 75 years and older, was led by the Albert Einstein College of Medicine in New York City, funded by the National Institute on Aging, and published in the New England Journal of Medicine. It calculated the percentage reduced risk of Dementia. The results were:
- 0% in bicycling, swimming or playing golf
- 35% in reading
- 47% in doing crossword puzzles at least four days a week
- 76% in dancing frequently

Quoting Doctor Joseph Coyle in 2003, A Harvard Medical School psychiatrist who wrote an accompanying commentary; "The cerebral cortex and hippocampus, which are critical to these activities, are remarkably plastic, and they rewire themselves based upon their use".

The only physical activity found to offer protection against dementia was frequent dancing.

Dancing is proven to:
- Reduce stress and depression
- Increase energy and serotonin
- Improve flexibility, strength, balance, endurance
- Strengthen bones and boosts cardiovascular health
- Increase mental capacity by exercising our cognitive processes
- Create new neural paths through Dynamic and rapid-fire decision making

According to a review in the *European Journal of Physical and Rehabilitation Medicine* in 2009, dancing may help people with Parkinson's disease, which is characterised by rigid muscles, slowed movement, and impaired balance.

The authors of a meta-analysis of 27 studies on the effectiveness of dance movement therapy, published in *Arts in Psychotherapy* in 2014, concluded that dancing should be encouraged as part of treatment for people with depression and anxiety.

From a 2013 article titled, "*The Neuroanatomical Correlates of Training-Related Perceptuo-Reflex Uncoupling in Dancers.*" The research suggests that years of training can enable dancers to suppress signals from the balance organs in the inner ear linked to the cerebellum. The findings, published in the journal *Cerebral Cortex*, could help to improve treatment for patients with chronic dizziness. Around one in four people experience this condition at some time in their lives.

A little saying found on Facebook that I had to include here:

When my soul is hurting DANCE makes me feel better
When I am overwhelmed DANCE helps me forget for a while
When I face struggles DANCE inspires me to keep going
When I lose confidence DANCE gives it back
I have been given one of the greatest gifts in the world... DANCE!

Where can you go to learn Line Dancing?

There are different styles of line dancing depending on where you go to learn. Each has their own unique theme and flavour. Not all of them will be available in your area, but they can be located and experienced if you are a curious traveller. The teaching and counting will likely be in the local language, but often the terminology to describe the choreography will be in English.

Bar/Pub Line Dancing

There are many bars and pubs that offer line dancing classes throughout the world. These bars are generally themed in nature, such as honkytonks or country and western themed. At these venues the instructors are generally required to use music that fits in with the theme of the venue.

Quite often these venues will cater for beginners and tourists that come in to get a taste of an authentic country bar. There will often be other forms of dance offered as well, such as two stepping and swing classes. The existence of these line dance classes will often be determined by the bar takings generated by the class, and may be shut down by the venue if it is determined that the class does not generate enough revenue.

If the bar caters for tourists, then the dances that are offered are likely to be very simple and lots of fun. As these customers are generally transient, it is difficult for the instructor to develop the abilities of individual dancers over time. The instructor will often have a short playlist of dance choreography to draw from and will repeat them from session to session or week to week.

In reality, serious line dancing and alcohol do not mix very well, so the difficulty level of dancing in bar line dancing is unlikely to get very high, and will likely drop as the level of intoxication of the participants increases.

Cruise Ship Line Dancing

Many cruise ship companies feature line dancing as part of their on-board activities. Cruise ships have a unique set of conditions that do not fit well with the traditional style of line dancing. The dance floors are small and often made of non-slip surfaces. The dancers are transient, so there is no development of abilities from class to class. The environment can be unstable with the rolling and pitching of the ship, even though it might be only gentle movement. The sessions are also generally short in length, often for only thirty minutes duration.

The cruise ship line dance teachers have adapted to this environment by developing choreography that involves a large degree of arm dancing (see definition later on), has avoided turns and twists, is quick and easy to teach, and utilises popular and catchy music to fit in with the various themes that are encouraged on cruises. The dancers are having fun, laughing a lot and are getting exercise.

Though many line dance purists would not consider that these are line dances, they still attract a lot of customers and are a very popular part of the ship's entertainment programme. The publicity for line dancing through this channel does assist in bringing new people into the more traditional club line dance environment when they return home all enthused.

Club Line Dancing

A line dance club is set up by an individual or organisation to specifically teach and dance line dancing. They hire a venue and conduct the class as they want. They are generally not required to fit any specific theme and can select the choreography and music that they want to teach themselves. This gives them the flexibility to control both the structure and the levels of the classes.

These line dance clubs often network together to provide a path to higher level dancing as the participants experience increases. Just make sure you pick a club that offers a specific beginners or entry level class to enable a gradual introduction to line dancing, rather than throwing you in the deep end with all the experienced dancers.

Line Dance Choreography Structure

A line dance is a repeating "sequence" of actions. Often there will be one or more turns during the sequence. These turns usually cause the next sequence to start facing another direction, called a wall. If a dance has no overall turn, then it is referred to as a one wall dance. If it has an overall turn of a half, it is referred to as a two wall dance. If it has an overall turn of a quarter, then it is referred to as a four wall dance.

Originally, most dances were done to any piece of music the instructor or dancer felt like using, or any song a live band might be playing at the time.

Over the years, as dancers became musically aware, and as choreographers became more knowledgeable, following the phrasing of the music became more important. Choreographers started to plan interruptions to the standard flow of the dance to match the music where needed.

A line dance will generally have a single sequence that repeats over and over, till the end of the music. Most songs are not that rigid in structure. Interruptions cause the dance to break that repeating structure, and do something else instead. This made dances more connected to very specific pieces of music, so less transferrable to other tunes.

There are a number of different types of interruptions that will be detailed later in the book. The most common are Restarts, Bridges and Substitutions. The others are far less common, but are occasionally used. A thoughtful choreographer will keep the amount of extra choreography to a minimum and may use the same extra piece of choreography as both a Bridge and a Substitution.

Dancing Technique for Line Dancing

Line dance technique and styling is very much a personal taste and cultural choice. Like every other popular dance community, there is a general social dance community and a competition and performance dance community.

The way competition ballroom dancers execute their steps bears little resemblance to the way that social ballroom dancers execute their steps at the local 60/40 dance hall. Social dancers are dancing for fun and social contact. Competition dancers are being judged against clear criteria of foot placement, stance and execution of timing. Furthermore the way that performance ballroom dancers execute their choreography bears little resemblance to the competition dancers. The focus of performance ballroom dancers is to provide a spectacle to entertain the audience rather than adhere to a strict regulation.

Line dancing has a similar spectrum of participants and celebrities. We have our local classes run by local instructors; we have our workshop weekends run by celebrity instructors. There are line dance competitions locally, nationally and internationally in many parts of the world. There are performance groups that present line dancing for television or corporate events. Each group of dancers need to decide what level of technique works for them and be happy with it.

Line Dance Style

In many countries when line dancing first started, the style of dancing was very "Yee Haah". Thumbs in belts, cowboy hats, boots and high impact jumps were all the rage. Arms were not used at all because the dance halls were so crowded that a waving arm could cause injuries.

When line dancing hit Asia, it was introduced by members of the ballroom dancing community. They developed a much more fluid style and incorporated many Latin and ballroom components both in music and technique. They introduced a lot more upper body and arm styling.

There is nothing in line dancing to say you have to use arms or styling, nor is there anything to say you can't. It is all about personal taste and style. Make your own style and be proud of it.

Just remember, line dancing is primarily about your feet, and where to put them.

Line Dance Etiquette

When dancing either in a class, or a social environment, there are a number of rules you should consider to show courtesy to your fellow dancers.

1. Never eat or drink, or carry food while on the dance floor. Should you spill anything on the floor, or on someone else, it could be dangerous.
2. Put your mobile phone on silent or vibrate so as not to interrupt other dancers.
3. If you must leave the dance floor while others are still dancing, get to the outside of the floor via the shortest route and then walk around the outside to your destination. Never through the middle or towards oncoming dancers.
4. If you are sharing the floor with other forms of dancing such as two stepping, line dance in the centre, to leave a track for the circle dancers around the outside of the dance floor
5. Never stand on the dance floor to talk, if the music or teaching has started, please vacate the floor.
6. If you are attempting to try a dance above your level at a social, keep to the edge of the dance floor, in case you need to sit out.
7. Accommodate the less confidant dancers in the inner part of the dance floor (especially in classes), rather than leaving them on the edge, unless they are obviously attempting something above their experience. Encourage and support them, you were a new dancer once.
8. Do not talk while the instructor is teaching.
9. You do not own any of the dance floor. If someone is in "your spot", move to another one.
10. If the floor is crowded take small steps and be careful of others.

11. If you bump into someone, it is courteous to apologise whether it is your fault or not.
12. Never walk through a line of dancers to cross the floor if a dance is in progress.
13. Start another line, if joining an existing one will make it too crowded.
14. Never start a different dance unless there is plenty of room and you sense it is acceptable to do so.
15. Always show appreciation. Applaud live acts, instructors and DJ's. They work hard for you.
16. Always respect your fellow dancer. If they get it wrong, don't tell them so. If they put you off, don't tell them so. Encourage them instead.

Music

Line dancers do not need to be musicians; however an understanding of the structure of music will help in understanding the choreography. Bear with me, as this could get a little technical.

In a simplistic form, most music can be described in beats, measures and phrases. A song or piece of music is made up of a number of phrases of music. In popular music these are usually a verse or chorus of the song.

When listening to dance music, there should be a distinctive beat underlying the song. This is called the pulse of the music, much like the heartbeat of a body. In some songs (like some bodies), this pulse is hard to find. The harder to find it is, the harder it is to dance to the song. This pulse will usually have a prominent (louder) beat, followed by a number of quieter beats. This is the basis of rhythm. A Rhythm is a pattern of loud and softer beats.

A "beat" can also be made up from a number of part beats. In music, a beat can be cut into smaller parts. From a dancer's perspective, we generally only consider half-beats, though some choreographers use quarter-beats to change a "feel" of a dance to match a specific ballroom dance or Irish dance rhythm. If we use a half beat, we call it an '&' beat ("And" beat). On the rare occasions that quarter beats are used, they are called the 'e' and 'a' beats. So a beat cut into 4 would be called 1e&a2e&a etc. A piece of choreography that uses part beats is often referred to as syncopated.

A "measure" is made up of a standard number of beats. In "Common Time" (called 4/4 time) a measure consists of four even length beats. In "Waltz Time" (called 3/4 time) a measure consists of three even length beats. Rarely some songs are made up of phrases with different length measures. An example of this is in the song "Strawberry Fields Forever" by the Beatles. This song has some common time phrases, and some waltz time phrases making it very challenging to choreograph a dance to.

A "phrase" is made up of a number of measures. The phrases in a song may be of differing numbers of measures and there may be shorter "bridges" of music between the phrases. Trying to "Phrase" a dance to a piece of music is often the biggest challenge for a choreographer, as they attempt to work around the structure of the music. There are also often "introductions" (Intro) and "endings" (Outro) in the music which may be choreographed separately. The square dance and Sequence ballroom dance community do not cope well with "bridges" in their music, so often commission their own musicians to produce evenly structured versions of popular tunes. Line dance choreographers cope with phrasing variations by creating various interruptions which will be documented further into the book.

The "tempo" of a piece of music describes the speed the music is being played at. It is usually measured in beats per minute (bpm). To get a quick estimate of the speed per minute of a piece of music, count the beats (pulse) for fifteen seconds and then multiply the amount by four. Popular music is not created specifically for dancing, so the tempo may change throughout the music, depending on the reliability of the timekeeper in the band (usually the drummer). The ballroom dance community prefer a more regulated beat, so they often get music produced by their own bands using "strict tempo", to make it more suitable for their dancing.

Sometimes a piece of music may have more than one dominant beat, making it difficult to determine the structure of the measures. Sometimes there is a really strong beat that seems a lot slower, but you can still count the fast beats. If you count the fast half beats then the speed may be determined as twice the speed of the actual music than when the slow primary beat is counted.

History of Line Dance Music

The origins of what we call line dancing today can be traced back through the disco music era of the seventies, to the late fifties with dances like "The Madison" from Columbus Ohio in 1957 which generated its own music to go to the dance.

Line dancing has been associated with country music from the early 1970's, and far more closely linked from the 1990s. Line dancing gained great exposure with the film clip to "Achy Breaky Heart" by Billy Ray Cyrus. Exposure was also generated in the film "Urban Cowboy" with John Travolta which featured both line dancing and two stepping scenes. These videos brought line dancing into the public eye and the line dance craze took off exclusively to country music. Most of the choreography was simple in construct, often favouring the left leg and was usually not targeted at a specific piece of music. You could do one dance to many pieces of music, or even a live band if the opportunity arose.

Progressively the choreography became more sophisticated and specific dances became commonly targeted at specific pieces of music. During the middle of the 1990's the definition of "Country" was stretched to cover country music artists doing non country cover songs, and country artists making it into the pop charts.

By the late 1990's Irish music was introduced to the line dance community with dances like "Coastin'". By the end of the 1990's choreographers were running out of new lively, country rock music, and were starting to utilise alternative music.

The Beach Boys' song "Still Cruisin'" was the first occasion I recall, where a non-country song was promoted as a line dance tune. It created quite a dilemma for us, and to avoid conflict, we decided to use "Fly like a Bird" by Boz Scaggs instead. Ironically he wasn't a country artist either, but somehow that song was accepted as country. The dilemma was extended when another popular dance came out to "Fly like a Bird", giving us our first "Split Floor" (2 dances done at the same time, one in the front and one down the back).

This did not sit well with some of the original line dance community. Major wars (well small skirmishes anyway) broke out over selection of dance music in some line dance establishments. Some teachers were staunch supporters of "Country Music Only". Others didn't want to use Country music at all, attempting to move away from the stigma of the "Billy Ray Cyrus" image. Some choreographers decided to provide two alternative pieces of music for their latest creations, one county and one non-country, just to keep everybody happy.

There was quite a resistance to Latin and Asian music in the early years as well. Many people were not happy if they couldn't understand the lyrics. In reality, some of the English language songs can't be understood either, so it shouldn't matter really. It is important to realise that line dancing is an international dance form, and many non-English speaking people are listening to English language songs, so what is the difference?

Fast forward to today when anything goes, for line dance music, even African, Latin, Celtic, Asian, Pop, Rap, Rock, Euro, Jazz, Opera, Classical; nothing is sacred to the line dance community. If a beat can be heard, and some repetitive structure can be found, then someone will try to choreograph a dance to it.

It is a shame that some in the line dance community completely shun country music line dances. History is history and it can't be changed, country music is a part of what line dancing is no matter what you call it. I believe country music dances should be cherished and promoted. Remember, you didn't create line dancing; you are just part of the overall line dance community.

There is one important observation to make when comparing the longevity of dances with respect to music selection. Pop tunes go out of fashion quicker than Country tunes seem to. So when a song goes out of fashion, often the dance that goes to it also loses popularity.

Body Mechanics

Though most line dance descriptions mention primarily foot placement, what the dancer does with his or her upper body is equally important. It is important to understand the concept of "Centre of Gravity" or COG. If you lean your upper body to the side or forward too far you will fall over. That is because you have moved your weight away from the foot that is supporting the weight, causing an imbalance.

Your head is usually the heaviest part of your body, so how far you move it will determine how fast you can return it. You naturally position your head to maintain proper balance.

If there is a sudden reversal of direction in a dance, often the upper body will be tilted or leaned to assist the smoothing of the choreography. This is generally not noted on the dance sheets.

Size of Step

Line dancing is done by individual people. Unlike ballroom dancing, there is no one else for them to hold on to, to keep their balance (not that you ever hang off your partner at any time). There may also be numerous changes of direction within a dance. For this reason step sizes should be small, slightly smaller than shoulder width apart. If the music is fast, then the steps should be smaller still. Sometimes line dance waltzes are choreographed to allow dancers to use larger steps, but not always.

Which way to Turn?

Many dancers cannot determine which way a Left" or a "Right" turn goes. If you put your nose over your left shoulder and chase it, you are doing a "Left" turn.

Watching your Feet

Many dancers make a habit of watching their feet. It is almost like they don't trust their brain to pass on the message. This will give bad posture and does not really help improve their dancing. Stop It! Remember, your head weighs approximately five kilograms which you are trying to push away from your body. This will create an imbalance.

What to Do with your Arms

When line dancing became really popular, the dance floors got really crowded. If people waved their arms around, they would invade the personal space of their adjacent dancers. They were therefore encouraged to stick their thumbs in their belts, or put their hands behind their backs or in their pockets.

As the dance floors have become less crowded, this is no longer necessary. Having movable arms actually helps create balance for the body, so assists comfortable dancing. Moving the arms around is good for creating upper body strength as well, so don't feel inhibited, express yourself, just don't hit people with them.

Feet Together Actions

When humans bring their feet together, the natural instinct is to distribute the weight evenly between both feet for comfort. For that reason the actions "close" and "touch" can be the most difficult to master for the inexperienced dancer. Until the weight distribution skills are mastered, movements like "coasters" and "montereys" will seem very difficult.

Locking Steps

If the choreographer calls for a locking movement after a forward or backward step, often the dancer will feel a sense of imbalance when trying to execute it. This is because the lock will cause the foot to move diagonally to get to the outside of the other foot. There is a technique to make that action comfortable for the dancer.

Rather than stepping directly forward or back on the step before the lock, step slightly across the other foot, with a very slight shoulder lead. This will allow the locking foot to move directly forward rather than on the diagonal, so not throwing the centre of gravity off.

Watching Other Dancers

Often the new dancer will get into the habit of watching those around them and copying the steps. This is a really bad mode of learning for them. There will be a delay between seeing another person's feet move, trying to work out what they did, and then sending the message to their own feet. By the time they have done this the other person's feet have moved again and they will always be playing catch-up and dancing a little late. Use other dancers to verify your actions, but make the actions using your own brain. You will make mistakes for a while, but they will be your mistakes.

Too many dancers cannot dance unless a certain someone is next to, or in front of them. If that person is sick or moves, they can no longer dance. That is not a good way to be. This leads to people having their "spot" on the floor, and ensuring others keep their "spots" too. It destroys any chance of new people being accommodated into the class.

Obviously it is important to watch the instructor, but be aware that the instructor will generally exaggerate their steps to make sure that the dancers down the back can see what they are doing. They do not expect you to also take such big steps as well. Keep the steps small while you learn to balance and turn.

What should I wear as a Dancer?

There are many schools of thought on what you should wear to line dance classes and socials. Often it is dependent on the weather conditions and the time of year. However there are some things that are constant.

Clothing

You will get warm while you are dancing. If you need warm clothes to get to the dance, make them layered, so you can peel the layers off as you warm up.

Often a dance group will have a "club shirt". If you get one of the shirts, it will stop you worrying about "what will I wear this week?"

Having a club shirt does not imply you know what you are doing. However if you can find one of the shirts with the micro-chip implant, with all the dance steps programmed in it, buy one. I haven't found one yet for me, but we can all hope they will be invented one day.

Footwear

The most common choices seen on the dance floor are:

- Sneakers – Can give too much grip, especially if moisture is in the air, but give good support to the sole of the foot.
- Cowboy Boots – Good support for the ankles but can be heavy and flatten your foot action.
- Dance Boots – Look like Cowboy Boots but are lighter and more flexible. Often made to measure and usually expensive and shouldn't be worn outside
- Flat street shoes – Can be abrasive on the floor
- Dance Sneakers – An unusual form of sneaker many people swear by
- Ballet flats/slippers – Tend to wear out quickly but are light and flexible
- Tap Shoes (without the taps) – Good heel and good support
- High Heels/Stilettos – Ok for ballroom dancing if you have a partner to support you, really really bad for line dancing.

The best footwear will be comfortable, offer good ankle support, and allow you to turn and spin easily, with a wide small heel. If you find too much grip is a problem, go to a shoe repairer and ask that they can glue "greenhide" on the sole. This will provide a better slip, even for sneakers. There are also "Shoe Socks" available to be worn outside of the shoe to reduce grip.

Just remember however, that if you use these modified shoes outside, the hide will quickly wear out. It is better to keep the shoes specially for dancing and change them when you get there and when you leave.

When you walk into the dance hall, please brush the grit off your footwear before entering. This grit when on the floor will create scratches and marks that could stop the venue owner from hiring the hall out.

Line Dance Specific Terminology

Line dancers have terminology they use to describe things that are important to them. I am not including the descriptions of the actual foot patterns here; they are in a later section of their own.

Class Specific Terms

Auto Pilot – Usually kicks in about two minutes into a song and is often associated with "Going Shopping". Your brain thinks everything is going well, so decides to go into automatic mode allowing for other distractions to kick in.

Classics – Dances that have been taught at least five years in the past, but that are still very popular on the dance floor in the present.

Going Shopping – This is the art of letting the mind wander while executing a dance. It does not often go well.

Golden Classics – Dances that have been taught at least ten years in the past, but that are still very popular on the dance floor in the present.

Log Book – When it comes to request time, often people forget the names of the dances they have done. Many dancers overcome this by keeping a log book. When they learn a new dance, they write the name of the dance in the book. Alongside the name of the dance they put an indicator of how much they liked the dance. This might be stars or ticks. The more there are, the better they liked it. They can then refer to this in class or at socials when thinking of requests.

Mistakes – There are no mistakes, only variations (or so they say).

Nemesis Dance – Some dancers have one dance that always troubles them. There is often no logic behind it, they just have a mind block.

Revision – Dances that have been done recently, or in the past, and are being revised to help keep them in the dancer's memory.

Teach – Detailed breaking down of the choreography with a high level or repetition, and thorough explanations.

Vanilla – Doing a dance exactly as a choreographer or instructor intended, without any options or variations.

Variations – A variation is a substitution of an alternative movement for the one that was originally intended. Usually they are deliberate, but sometimes not.

Walk Through – Far less detailed than a teach, with an assumption made that the dancers have already done the dance previously and just need a reminder. Possibly only one or two sequences will be covered.

Event Specific Terms

Class – A regular line dance function that has been set up to teach line dancers in a slow, detailed and repetitive manner.

Social – A less regular line dance function that has been set up to give the dancers the chance to experience their favourite dances without spending time teaching them again. Often a social will "walk through" dances as a reminder, but not teach them, however many have no walk through at all. Sometimes the social will be run by request from the audience, other times pre-programmed by the Instructor conducting the Social.

Workshop – A workshop is a line dance function set up to celebrate an event, or to gather a group of dancers together to experience something out of the ordinary. Often it would feature an instructor that has been invited to the event as a guest instructor. This guest will teach a number of dances, either of their design, or at least of their selection to those present.

Split Floor – A split floor occurs when a piece of music is played, and more than one piece of choreography is done to it at the same time. This usually happens in Socials. It may occur when a hard dance and an easy dance have been deliberately taught, to enable both experienced and newer dancers to experience the same music. It also may occur when two line dance groups are at the social and both have learnt a different dance to the same music. I have seen five way splits at some larger socials, which can be absolute chaos. Each dance will have a separate section of the floor, as they will likely have completely different traffic patterns and the dancers would collide.

No Man's Land – The space between the split floor dances. This space needs to be big enough to allow the two choreographies to stay separated. Often an instructor may be there to prevent the newer dancers from being distracted or invaded by the other dance.

Non-Technical Dance Descriptions

There are many ways to technically describe a particular piece of line dance choreography. However, each dance creates a sensation, which describes how the dance feels to a dancer while learning or doing the dance. These are not descriptions for the difficulty of the dance, because measuring difficulty is very dependent on the experience of the individual attempting the dance. Here are a few of them:

- Busy – Lots of & count actions so the dance is full of action
- Complex – Lots of structure with interruptions or phrasing
- Dizzy – Lots of turns in the same direction
- Jerky – Lots of abrupt changes of direction
- Jumpy – Lots of jumps and high impact actions
- Leggy – Lots of kicks, points and touches
- One Legged – Seems to favour one leg over the other
- Smooth – All the steps seem to flow into one another
- Timing – Lots of Holds, or random use of many & counts
- Turny – Lots of turns, one after the other
- Twisty – Lots of twisting actions

Arm Dancing

Arm Dancing is choreography that involves using the arms and hands, often without any movement of the feet. Some dances such as "Larger than Life" (Ward) incorporate arm dancing to hit a particular feature in the music. Dances like "The Macarena" involve mainly arm dancing. Bollywood films show a lot of dancing that involves a large amount of arm dancing.

Though these dances are not usually thought of as line dancing, they still meet the definition of line dancing and like many other forms of dance are used as inspiration by line dance choreographers. Use of culturally or socially characteristic arm movements such as Egyptian arms, John Travolta points, or Thai finger clasps can add a theme to a dance, to match the style of the music chosen by the choreographer.

Humble Scale of Dancer Levels

I found this on Facebook and couldn't help including it here. These are some humorous but poignant definitions of levels of dancers (not serious definitions):

1. Beginner Dancer: Knows nothing
2. Intermediate Dancer: Knows everything, but is too good to dance with beginners
3. Hotshot Dancer: Too good to dance with anyone
4. Advanced Dancer: Dances everything, especially with beginners

Choosing a Class

As a dancer, or potential dancer, choosing where you go to dance can be important. You may not have a choice, depending on where you live, but if you do, you might want to consider the following issues:

- Who will cover your costs should you get injured while participating in, or attending the activity?
- Does your teacher have the necessary knowledge and skills to teach you properly and safely?

- Is your teacher a responsible member of the music community with the necessary licences to conduct the activity legally?
- Is your teacher a responsible member of the line dance community, and contribute to the overall progress of line dancing through associations or networks?
- Does your teacher cater appropriately for dancers of your experience level, and offer opportunities for advancement as you improve, should you want it?
- Does your teacher appropriately cater for and encourage learners for the long term future of the line dance community?
- Do they have public liability insurance?

There should be no reason why you cannot ask your teacher about these, or any other, issues should you be concerned. If they cannot answer your questions to your satisfaction, then it is your decision to stay or leave. Just remember that all of these responsibilities come at a cost to a teacher. If you are not paying very much for the class, then either someone is financially sponsoring the class, or you may not be getting a quality product.

If there are multiple choices around, it is worth while checking out all of them, and do this as early as possible before you become too used to one type of teaching. Each instructor has a different personality and style, some will suit you and others won't. If the first one isn't right, look for a better fit to your requirements, rather than giving up on the activity all together. Make sure you make the decision based on your own choice, rather than listening to other people's opinions. Each individual has their own requirements, abilities and tastes and therefore should make their own decisions.

Going to Socials

Once you have become a competent line dancer at whatever level you are dancing, the next phase of your dancing may be attending a local social. This can be quite scary, but also enlightening. You get to see what dancers at other levels are doing, and may even get to try out a few dances that are outside your classes play list. If the social you go to is being put on by an instructor other than your own, don't be a vocal critic. If you don't like it; just don't go back.

Try not to get in the way of other dancers, but try as much as you feel comfortable. Take your log book along with you, so you can put in some requests of your own. Don't put down other people's requests, make them your own.

Describing Line Dance Choreography

Line dancing started long before the digital age of the internet, laptop computers and music downloads. Dances were distributed on the back of napkins by someone scrawling notes about something they saw at a bar somewhere. The "Chinese whisper syndrome" was rife. Most choreography was written by "Unknown" and so the correct steps were unclear and unable to be traced. By the time a dance had gone from one side of a country to another it had morphed into something quite different so many variations developed.

People made up their own terminology based on their local language and experience, or what they thought they heard someone else say. For example: Butterflies became Buttermilks. Grapevines became Freezes because that was the name of the dance that used the step.

It is important to note that we are attempting to describe the moving flowing action of dancing to music, with a series of snapshot descriptions. It is like describing a movie using a series of photographs. It will never describe all of the subtle changes of position and weight, or the natural flow from one step to another. A balance must be made between completeness of description, and efficiency of information transfer. Ideally a dance description needs to fit on one page of text.

Dance Sheets

The distribution of line dance choreography is done primarily by paper, or the digital version of this, the text document. This "Dance Sheet" should contain information about who choreographed the dance, what music to use, and how and when to execute the steps. These sheets have various names throughout the line dance community, such as: Step sheet, Cue sheet, Dance Description, Script etc.

Generally down the left hand side of the sheet will be information about the timing and beat counts of the individual moves.

The execution part will usually be broken into "chunks", often of eight or more beats.

Each chunk will be described in detail, including the timing for the moves. These are called the "Detailed Description". Above that detail, will usually be an abbreviated description often referred to as the "Head Cues".

Up until now, the language used to describe both the "Detailed Description" and the "Head Cues" is completely arbitrary with no rules or standard. It is based solely on the experience and language of the person who created the sheet.

The overall style and layout of the rest of the dance sheet is also uncontrolled and arbitrary in structure. Some of the web site distributors of the sheets impose some structure on the submitted sheets, but the content is completely uncontrolled.

This lack of standards means there is no continuity of information from dance to dance, or choreographer to choreographer. The same steps may have different names and even different ways to describe them, even though the choreographic outcome is identical.

Legacy dances that are already in existence will always have this issue, but hopefully into the future, this book may assist in bringing a standard together for everyone's benefit.

History of Line Dance Sheets

Napkin Net

In the heyday of country line dance following the introduction of the song Achy Breaky Heart (and the line dance created to help market that song), new line dances were passed around in the most fundamental way possible;

word-of-mouth. As a new dance was created and taught, the dancers would write down the steps on whatever was handy (usually a bar napkin), and then use those hastily scribbled notes to teach the dance to their friends, and at other venues. There was no standard format or language for step sheets.

Book Net

Enterprising choreographers and instructors realised the need for documented dances, and started creating booklets of dance sheets for sale to the public. Many of them would sell their services to run regional workshops to teach a selection of dances that they had collected, and they would sell a manual of the step sheets to go with the event. Often they would be created in a standard layout hand typed by the presenter to improve the professionalism of the product.

Other organisations created magazines and newsletters with dance sheets attached, to help promote local choreographers, renowned choreographers or to share locally popular dances. These sheets were often joined by local news of events, or information about line dance personalities.

One early monthly national magazine was "Country Dance Lines" published in Woodacre, California, USA. In July 1984, Country Dance Lines started with eight pages. By 1995 it averaged over one hundred and ten pages. Many of those pages contained descriptions of dance steps and choreographed dances, most of which were line dances. In 1998 the magazine listed over three thousand, three hundred instructors across all states of the USA and sixteen other countries, including Australia, England, Canada, France, Germany, and even Saudi Arabia. In the year 2000 at the time that it ceased publication, it included over twenty two thousand subscribers and had catalogued over five thousand line and partner dances.

In June 1996, line dancing was so popular in England that a magazine simply titled Linedancer was launched. It remained a monthly print publication until November 2015. The digital version continued on till October 2016, when it too stopped publication due to lack of financial support.

Most of these publications have been abandoned because of the availability of online material.

In the early years, a few instructors attempted to produce a series of videos and eventually DVDs. These were briefly popular, but the delays in production and distribution meant that, by the time the product was ready for market, the dances being presented were out of fashion and wouldn't sell.

Also in the early days, some choreographers got annoyed that other instructors were making money from their creations and attempted to copyright their dances. The intent was to make people pay a licence fee to teach, or even dance their dances. It was found that it was impossible to police, and people just stopped doing the copyrighted dances. The concept was quickly abandoned.

USENET

In the early days of the internet, before the World Wide Web, there was something called USENET. It was like a modern discussion forum, except messages were read using a program called a newsreader (rather than a browser, which was not yet invented). There was no colour, sound, or graphics; just plain text on a plain background.

USENET was made up of thousands and thousands of news groups covering every subject imaginable, including several for line dancing. Anyone at all was allowed to join any newsgroup and immediately begin asking questions and joining into discussions. It was highly recommended that new members wait a few weeks to join into discussions, and that they read the USENET message archive to see what had already been discussed in the past. Those who ignored this advice were called "newbies". Newbies were notorious for asking questions that had already been asked and answered many times in the past. Eventually, someone would gather these questions into a single collection called a "Frequently Asked Questions" (or FAQ) page. If a FAQ existed, newbies were asked to read the FAQ before posting.

The FAQ for the group "Line & Country & Western Dance & Music" was created in 1995 by several people, headed up by Pete McCracken. A huge list of Individual Contributors is found in the FAQ itself.

The Table of Contents for one of the few remaining versions of the FAQ is found at http://haruff.ca/dance_faq/CONTENTS.HTM

It begins with a list of 25 or so USA-based choreographers, plus a few more from the UK and Australia. It then goes into music speeds, suggestions on writing step sheets, and so on. Eventually it gets to a collection of step sheets, presented in a rudimentary text format. This was the first online collection of step sheets.

World Wide Web

Soon after USENET became ubiquitous, the World Wide Web was introduced. Pages were viewed using a program called a browser and could include graphics, sound, and unlimited links to other pages. This quickly proved to be the preferred method for step sheet distribution. There was still no standard format, though webmasters of step sheet websites might include suggestion for those submitting step sheets.

In the early days of the Web, pages could simply link to other pages, so searching for step sheets involved working your way through a hierarchy of pages, perhaps with step sheets arranged alphabetically by title.

The biggest line dance website at this time was Information Super Dance Floor run by Don Deyne. Others included

- Ronald & Sandra's Dance Club Step Sheet Collection
- CW Line Dance Exchange - PDF format Step Sheet Collection
- Mustang Lone Star Dance Step Sheet Collection
- Line Dance Fun - PDF Format Step Sheet Collection
- Knox Rhine's Step Sheet Collection
- Cactus Star Dance Step Sheet Collection

And of course, Kickit. When line dancing became huge in the UK, they were quickly joined by Linedancer Magazine with their website.

Those with sites cooperated closely and shared danced willingly. As a new dance appeared on one site, it quickly migrated to the others. At this time there were about 2000 line dances making the rounds.

Eventually the folks who controlled the Web came up with ways to include forms on pages, so that visitors could do searches of a site by typing what they were looking for rather than clicking around until they found it.

Kickit was the first to use this new search method on a step sheet website, and it proved quite successful. The technology then began to show up on other sites.

Unusual Line Dance Choreography Structures

One thing is certain. Line dancing is a unique form of dance. It is only limited by the imagination of the choreographer and the willingness of the dancer to "give it a go". This has led to many unique "experimental" line dance creations over the years.

Some of the unique (and often unpopular) structures are:

- Sequenced Line Dances: Dances that have multiple parts in a specific sequence such as for example a dance that has 4 parts named A, B, C and D, and is done for example in the order of AABACAADCBA
- Mirrored Line Dances: Dances that execute a sequence of steps to finish on the other foot, then repeat the whole dance starting on the other foot.
- One Wall Line Dances: Dances that restart to the front every time. These dances can get very boring.
- 3 Wall Line Dances: Dances that restart to the front before the fourth wall is ever done.
- Blended Line Dancers: Two popular dances are done one after the other to make a longer dance.
- Wall Swap Dances – Occasionally a dance is written that is a two wall dance, using front and back, but when it is interrupted, it swaps

to using the side walls. Later on it may swap back again. It can also be a one wall dance that swaps to a different wall.
- Short dances to long music.
- Very, very long dances that repeat only a couple of times before the end of the music. These really are more performance dances than line dances.
- Dances with multiple bridges and hardly any "standard" sequences.

Limitations of Line Dance Choreography

There are some logical limitations to what is practical on a line dance floor. These were very evident when we had enormous crowds in small venues.

Line dancing is performed by multiple dancers with restricted space to execute the choreography. Any choreography that travels too far will not be practical in a crowded environment.

Line dancers do not have a partner to provide balance, so the actions must allow the dancer to keep their own balance while executing the action.

Standard amounts of turn are important to enable the dancers to align themselves to their environment. The smallest turn increment should be 1/8 to be practical. Any smaller turn is not noticeable to the average dancer, and finding a reference point in the hall, for the dancers in class, would be nearly impossible for the instructor.

Traditionally a dance will commence facing the front of the dance venue, though this is not always the case.

Choreography Terminology

Line dance choreography terminology is forever evolving. Because of the dynamic nature of the dance form, the words we use to describe need to be clear and concise in meaning, otherwise they may be misinterpreted. Unfortunately the English language has many meanings for the same words, and many words spelt differently that sound the same.

As line dancing has both a written and spoken dance "language", it is important that the words are not "overloaded" with too many meanings. It is also important not to use words that sound similar as they may be misheard. Typical overloaded words are "Left" and "Right". They can be used to select which foot, to select which positional direction and to select which rotational direction all at the same time. For example: Sweep the Right Toe to the Right and turn ¼ Right. Another overloaded word is Roll, sometimes referring to hands, hips, turning and even body rolls. We need to avoid overloading words when possible. Even the word "And" has multiple meanings especially in reference to music as well.

Some classic quotes that highlight this issue are:
- "Go back to the front" (should use the word return instead of go back)
- "Recover back to your left" (should use recover on your left)
- "Recover to your right" (ambiguous, should be recover on your right)
- "Facing forward" (where else can you face, try facing front)
- "Everybody right with that" (Is everybody OK with that)

Living Terminology

The important thing to realise about line dancing is that it is a dance form that drives terminology, rather than one that is driven by terminology.

Many other dance forms have a clearly defined set of rules and descriptions and techniques. People are then measured against those standards to determine their competence, and may be presented with medals for completing goals, or satisfying criteria. The rules govern the dancing.

Line dancing is the reverse of that. Choreographers come up with strange new actions and moves, and it is up to the line dance community to determine if they like the concept, and if so to give it a name. Line dance terminology therefore develops and grows over time.

I could not have created this book twenty years ago, as the dance form was not sufficiently mature. It is only now reaching a point where the need for consistency and standardisation is becoming an issue internationally. If I wrote this book in twenty years' time, it would look quite different I am sure.

What is so important about having Standard Terminology?

If you are not yet passionate about your line dancing, then you might want to skip this section. I'm about to stand on a soapbox for a couple of minutes. Don't say that I didn't warn you.

So many people over the years have criticised me for insisting that standard terminology is the way of the future. Their argument is that "it's not broke, so why fix it?" Their dancers are able to dance just fine without it. Why am I so convinced that I am right and they are wrong? What gives me the right to think that my way is best, and theirs is not? Isn't that just being conceited and pompous of me? Why can I see it and they cannot? Let me explain.

I run a large network of classes throughout my state. We have many instructors and many dancers that dance with multiple instructors. Some of the instructors we see rarely, others very frequently. We have many joint activities that span multiple instructors and classes. Our instructors travel widely, both within our country and abroad. Our dancers travel widely within our state, and compare the regional classes with the metropolitan classes. We network with many choreographers, instructors and dancers world-wide to gather the best possible material for our dance classes. We all attend regular training workshops to ensure we provide the best possible quality of product to our customers. We want to be the best we possibly can be. We can see that the current system is broken, because we are looking at the complete picture, not just one little pixel.

My dream has always been to create the "McDonalds" of line dancing. If a person wants to line dance I want us to be the place they first think of to go for their fix. Not ballroom dancing, not the Madison, not the Macarena, but progressive, modern, up to date line dancing. If you are anywhere in the world and crave a burger, then the first place you think of is McDonalds. What is so great about McDonalds? You walk into any McDonalds store world-wide and you will feel comfortable. The décor is the same, the food has the same taste, texture and look, the uniforms are the same, and the service is the same. You know what you are going to get, not Chinese food, not an Indian curry, not a Kebab. You will get a burger. The formula works and it will work anywhere in the world. When you are travelling in an unfamiliar country for any period of time, you hang out for a McDonalds just to taste the familiar food.

So what is it I am actually proposing? I propose that the industry needs:
- Standard content and layout of dance sheets
- Standard descriptions of the individual actions described on the dance sheets
- Standard description of the timing for the individual actions
- Standard descriptions of interruptions (bridges and restarts etc.)
- Standard descriptions of class level
- Standard meanings for the words that we use to describe things
- Standard terminology to describe the common clusters of steps
- Standard terminology to describe the timing of the common clusters of steps
- Standard terminology that is adaptive to accommodate unforeseen variations
- Standard methods to describe the count in of the music that we use
- Standard methods to get the dancers actually moving at the same time
- Standard methods for instructors to use to get the message across
- Standard methods to measure and describe the degree of difficulty of individual dances
- Standard methods to judge dancers, and choreography for competitions
- Standard methods to judge instructors for hiring for workshops and events

So let me explain the advantages of having these standards.

If dance sheet layout and content is standard, then searching for something in a database, either someone else's or your own, is simplified. No longer do you need to go hunting for missing information. It allows for content checker programmes to be made available to confirm the existence of the content, before submitting it to the distribution network. This also allows an easier transition from paper based dance sheets to electronic tablet based dance sheets when you are ready to take the leap.

Standard descriptions of moves allow a translator programme to be created to convert any dance sheet written in English to be translated into French, Mandarin, Spanish and any other language at the press of a button.

Standard description and meanings of actions, timing and interruptions will reduce the occurrence of misinterpretation from both instructors and dancers, and allow everyone world-wide to be dancing the same way, without having to compare videos, making guesses and defending decisions. It allows a parser programme to be developed to proof read dance sheets before they are published. It allows an anime programme to be developed to simulate dancers performing a dance before it has been published, enabling the comfort and flow of the dance to be improved before subjecting the choreography to real people.

Standard terminology allows experience gathered from one dance and one teacher to be reused in other dances and other classes without fear of ambiguity. It allows evaluation programmes to be developed to automatically calculate the difficulty of dances before they have been published, or even danced.

Standard teaching and operational methods allow instructors to improve their skills and compare their abilities with their peers. It allows the dancers to be more mobile, internationally and regionally with confidence that they will be able to understand, no matter where they dance, and no matter what language the actual teaching is conducted in.

Standard methods of judging competitions allows for smoother events and less friction between judges, event coordinators and competitors. It allows for more integration between events, both nationally and internationally.

Doesn't that sound like a future line dance world you would want to be part of?

Heath Line Dance Choreography Model

Here is terminology syntax for describing a line dance. A more detailed description will follow.

- Do something + with something + where = Action
- Type of turn + how much + which way = Turn
- Turn + Action + Action + ... + Turn = Move
- Move + Move + ... + Timing = Cluster
- Cluster + Cluster + ... = Chunk
- Chunk + Chunk + ... + Interruptions = Choreography
- Choreography + Music = Dance
- Venue + Dancers + Instructor + Dance + Dance + ... = Class

Terminology Structure

Line dancing activity can be thought of as a pyramid of descriptions. At the bottom of the pyramid are the "actions".

Each "action" involves a single part of the body and a single activity, such as "step the right foot forward", or "clap the hands".

There might be only one action, or multiple actions that make up a "move", but all of those actions must happen at exactly the same time. So for example: "step the right foot forward and clap the hands" is two actions, but it is one "move". Each "move" should have a key word or two that describes, or abbreviates the move. For the previous example, that example move could be called: "Forward & Clap".

A "Move" may also incorporate some turning. A "Turn" can happen either before an action, or after an action. It cannot happen between the actions; otherwise they wouldn't be done at the same time. If that were the case, they should be described as two separate "Moves" on different parts of the beat.

There may be many actions being done at a time with different parts of the body. For example we can Twist a heel and Hitch the other knee and Slap the hitched knee with a hand and Click the fingers of the other hand all at the same time (you probably wouldn't want to, but it is possible). That would make a very complex move, but it is still one move.

If we put multiple "Moves" together, we get a "Cluster". So if there were four of the previous example "Forward & Clap" moves, one after the other, on separate beats of music, we would call that Cluster "Run 4 with Claps".

Action Terminology

A "Hold" is a very special action. It means do not do anything with your feet. Don't transfer weight, don't move them, do nothing. It can be a very difficult action for newer dancers to achieve, as they want to do something on every beat. If there are more than four holds in a row, you can assume a dancer will probably have transferred the weight to both feet by the end of the holds. Most dancers don't like standing on one foot for very long.

Any other action description should contain the following information in the given order:

- Size of Action: such as small or large, if regular size is not wanted.
- Name of Action
- Which part of the body: Left, Right or Both
- What part of the body: Hand, Foot, Toe etc.
- Direction of Action (occasionally not needed)
- If Needed: Which Associated part of the body for the action: Left, Right or Both
- If Needed: What Associated part of the body for the action

An associated part is a second part of the body used for the action. For example "Slap the Right Knee" is incomplete, as it doesn't mention which hand to slap the knee with. A more complete description would be: "Slap the Right Knee with the Left Hand". In this example a direction was not needed.

Direction Terminology

Obviously the words Left and Right are used to describe directions. There are other words that help clarify the intended placement of the foot. A direction will describe where to go between each individual move. As soon as a move is complete, then the next direction will describe moving from that new position, not from some previous position.

- Apart – Usually used when describing landing from a jump. ie: jump feet apart
- Back – Directly back from the body
- Behind – Is a crossing direction behind the body
- Centre – Directly under the body
- Closer – Not alongside but closer than it was
- Diagonal – Creates the opportunity to combine two directions such as Diagonal Forward and Left
- Forward – Directly forward of the body
- Front/Cross – Is a crossing direction in front of the body
- Further – Extends a previous direction, as in point further forward
- In – Towards the centre
- Inline – Foot is directly one in front of the other
- On the Spot – Directly under the body usually for multiple moves over multiple beats.
- Out – Away from the centre
- Past – Passes the other foot, either passing forward or passing back
- Slightly – Creates the opportunity to reduce the size of the direction, such as Diagonal Forward and Slightly Left
- Tightly – Is closer than is usually comfortable
- Towards – Is not there yet, as in draw towards (but not there yet)

There are other words that are used to describe upper body actions such as "Low", "High", "Up", "Down", "Above" and "Below".

Turn Terminology

If the turn is associated with an action, it is important to understand the order of events. This is because misinterpretation could cause a different outcome. For example: "Turn ½ and step forward" will cause the body to move back from its original position, whereas "step forward and turn ½" will cause the body to move forward from its original position. This is the difference between a "Pre Turn" (a turn before the action) and a "Post Turn" (a turn after the action). Because dancers may be tightly packed on a dance floor, this misinterpretation could cause collisions.

There are a number of words that help describe the various types of "turns" that are used in line dancing as well as the standard word "Turn". I try to avoid the word "Turning", as it is a bit vague regarding when to do the turn, either before, or after the actions.

- Circle – Used to describe a series of actions that move the body in an arc. The circle will be either clockwise or anti-clockwise in direction (for those with only digital time awareness this may be an education for you). Left or Right should not be used to describe this type of turn as it could be executed with either foot, so the use of Left or Right would be too overloaded when being described.
- Commence – Start the required turn, but don't do all of it
- Complete – Finish the already started turn
- Continue – Continue the already started turn but don't complete it
- Gradual – A gradual turn is a turn executed over a number of actions. The amount of actions it takes to execute the turn can be described using the Commence, Complete and Continue terms.
- Unwind – The legs remain where they are (already crossed) and the heels are lifted and the knees straightened to complete the desired amount of turn to completely or partially uncross the legs. After an Unwind, a decision needs to be made which foot will be made available, as either or both are possible.
- Wind – The legs remain where they are (Usually uncrossed) and the heels are lifted and knees slightly bent to complete the desired amount of turn to completely or partially cross the legs. It is important to know which way to wind however, as either is possible.

Parent Actions

This is a list of the common fundamental actions done with the lower parts of the body.

- Bend – As you would expect.
- Brush – Briefly contacting the floor with the toe of the foot in a passing motion. If no direction is specified it is forward
- Bump – A movement of the hip with a change of weight
- Draw – Bringing the foot towards the other foot
- Drop – Dropping part of the foot or body
- Flare – Swinging the foot in an arc above the floor without touching it.
- Flick – Lift the Foot up by bending the knee without lifting the knee. If no direction is specified it is up and out.
- Hop – Keeping the weight on the same foot vigorously flex the knee to lift the whole body off the floor
- Jump – Vigorously flexing both knees to lift the whole body off the floor
- Leap – Vigorously flexing the knee to lift the whole body off the floor and transfer the weight to the other foot
- Lift – lifting part of the foot or body
- Recover – Return of weight from a rock, usually to where the foot originated
- Rock – Move the foot with partial weight change. The other foot will still have some weight on it so usually cannot be moved. In some circumstances it can be moved, but will be done very quickly before the dancer falls over.
- Scuff – Briefly contacting the floor with the heel of the foot in a passing motion. If no direction is specified it is forward
- Slide – Move the foot along the floor without losing contact with the floor and then change weight
- Stamp – Vigorously strike the foot to make noise but don't change weight. If no direction is specified it is "On the Spot".
- Step – Move the foot with full weight change. The other foot will have no weight on it now, so is available for any other action.

- Stomp – Vigorously strike the foot to make noise and fully change weight. If no direction is specified it is "On the Spot".
- Straighten – Undoing a bend.
- Sway – A movement of the whole body with a change of weight
- Sweep – Swinging the foot in an arc in contact with the floor.
- Touch – Move the foot with no weight change. If no direction is specified it is alongside the other foot and if no part of the foot is specified, at least the ball of the foot actually touches the floor.
- Transfer – Changing the weight to another or both feet
- Twist – Turning of part of the foot such as the heel or toe or parts of both feet, knee or torso etc.

There are also many actions associated with the upper body and hands such as: Clap, Click, Slap, Look, Shake, Wave etc.

Derived Actions

A derived action refers to a parent action, but also has more specific execution or placement information.

- Aerial – A Lift of a straight leg forward in an upward arc with a pointed toe.
- Close – A Step, but it is alongside the inside of the other foot.
- Cross – A Step, but it is across the other foot, either behind or in front
- Dig – A Touch with the heel, but using a bent knee, like when pushing a spade into the earth. If no direction is specified it is forward
- Drag – A Draw, but with the heel rather than the toe or flat foot
- Heel – A forward Touch of the heel
- Hitch – A Lift of the Knee. If no direction is specified it is straight up
- Kick – A Lift of the foot with a straight leg and toe up. If no direction is specified it is forward
- Lock – A Step, but the knees lock in behind each other enabling the foot to close along the outside of the foot rather than the inside of the foot. It may be in front, or behind.
- Point – A touch of the toe with a straight leg and ankle with no body weight. If no direction is specified it is to the side

- Skate – A slide, but is done in a curving manner forward and then out, or back and then out.
- Tap – A Touch with the toe, but using a bent knee and a raised heel, usually across behind, or across in front, of the other foot
- Toe – A back Touch of the toe

Combined Actions (multiple actions at the same time)

There are some common actions that when put together make a distinctive combined action.

- Pop – A three action combination of:
  - bending one knee; and
  - straightening the other; while
  - transferring weight from one foot to the other.
- Strut – A two action combination of:
  - dropping part of the foot (either heel or toe) while
  - transferring the weight. (see Note 1)
- Grind – A two action combination of:
  - a twist of the lifted toe with the heel of the same foot still on the floor and
  - a transfer of weight from one foot to the other. (see Note 2)

Note 1: Be aware that a "Point Forward, Step Forward" is not executed the same way as a "Point Forward, Strut". When executing a Strut, the toe does not lose contact with the floor and the weight is rolled onto that foot dropping the heel. When executing a Step, the foot is lifted completely off the floor and then lowered to the floor again.

Note 2: There are two variants of this. The First and most common is a Twist combined with a Recover onto the other foot which is considered a "Grind". The second is a Twist combined with a transfer to the same foot which is considered a "Grinding Strut". Both start with the toe already turned in, and the twist action is outward.

Move Terminology

Move terminology is used to provide short abbreviation words for the actions in the move. Most actions are uncomplicated steps in a simple direction, so those terms are kept simple, because they are used most. More complicated actions will create more words in the move description, but they are used much less often, so can be tolerated.

Here are some common examples that are used further on:
- Step Right Foot to Right = Side
- Cross Left Foot Behind Right Foot = Behind
- Cross Left Foot in Front of Right Foot = Front
- Step Left Foot Forward = Forward
- Step Left Foot Back = Back
- Step Left Foot Diagonal Forward and Left = Diagonal Forward
- Touch Left Foot to Right Foot = Touch
- Close Left Foot to Right Foot = Close
- Rock Right Foot Forward = Forward Rock
- Recover Left Foot = Recover
- Bump Right Hip Forward = Bump Forward
- Point Left Toe to Left = Point
- Point Left Toe Forward = Point Forward
- Lock Right Foot Behind Left Foot = Lock
- Lock Right Foot in Front of Left Foot = Lock (only one will be logical, so no need to distinguish)
- Rock Left Foot Across in Front of Right Foot = Cross Rock
- Rock Left Foot Behind Right Foot = Behind Rock

The order of words is important as they are used for verbal cues to the dancers. "Forward Rock" is better than "Rock Forward", because the dancer can start moving forward before they need to know what they are doing forward. Bump Forward is better than Forward Bump, because the foot is not moved in this case, so we don't want to encourage a move of the foot.

Cluster Terminology

A "Cluster" is a series of moves over a number of beats or part beats. These can be quite simple, but also can be very complex. New clusters are being invented all the time as they are "recycled" from other dance forms. Also combinations that are used frequently eventually get given a name to ease instruction time.

Clusters can be grouped into families. There may be a parent cluster, and then associated with that are a number of other clusters. These other clusters are of a similar or related structure, but modified in some way to be slightly different. These modifications can be documented using modifying terms.

Cluster Punctuation

In making the following descriptions I have distinguished separate timing with comma punctuation. There may be more complex punctuation when a dance sheet is created. I have used the letter "H" to signify a Hold for timing purposes.

Parent Line Dance Clusters

It is important that each cluster has a standard set of moves, turns and just as importantly timing. These parents may then be varied to create other similar moves with slightly different names.

Applejack – Twist the toe of one foot in a direction and twist the heel of the other foot in the same direction, on the next beat return the twisted parts to their original place. Timing is 1&

Basketball (Pivot) – Forward Rock, Turn ½ and Recover where the turn is towards the recovering foot, timing is 1,2. For example with your right foot rock forward, then turn ½ left and recover on the left foot. The word Pivot has been used for so many different actions in the past that I avoid it to save confusion. It is easier to say than Basketball, and provided it is used for half turns only, it is an acceptable word for this cluster.

Box – "Side, Close, Forward, Touch, Side, Close, Back, Touch" with timing 1,2,3,4,5,6,7,8

Chasse (Sha-Say) – Chasse is a series of "Side, Close, Side, Close" moves with timing 1,2,3,4. If no number is specified it will be 3 moves starting from the first Side, but always to the side first.

Coaster – "Back, Close, Forward". Commonly a Coaster uses only these three moves with timing of 1&2, but if there is a fourth move in a Coaster variant, it will be a Close.

Fan – "Twist the toe out, Twist the toe in" (Can also be done with the heel to be a "Heel Fan") timing is 1,2

Front Vaudeville – Effectively a Vaudeville but starting in a different move: "Front, Side, Diagonal Heel, Side" with timing 1&2&

Grind – Is a "Forward Rock, Recover", but the toe is turned in on the slightly overweighted Rock and as the Recover is executed, the Toe is turned Out, causing the Heel to "Grind" on the floor. Timing is 1,2 and the number of counts must be specified.

Heel Drops – A sequence of lifting and dropping the heel (or both heels), with timing &1

Heel Jack – "Back, Heel, Forward, Touch" with the timing &1&2

Hip Walk – "Diagonal Forward and Bump Forward, Bump Back, Bump Forward" with timing 1&2

In In – "Step centre, Close" timing is &1

Jazz Box – "Front, Back, Side, Forward" with timing 1,2,3,4. It takes the shape of a square on the floor, thus the name Box.

Kay Step – Diagonal Forward, Touch, Diagonal Back, Touch, Diagonal Back, Touch, Diagonal Forward, Touch, with timing 1,2,3,4,5,6,7,8. I have added the "ay" to make the K easier to be noticed in documentation.

Montana Kick – "Forward, Kick, Back, Point Back" with timing 1,2,3,4

Monterey – "Point, Turn ½ and Close, Point, Close" with timing 1,2,3,4 and turning in the direction of the first pointed toe. Unless specified differently, it will be a ½ turn. Usually starting using the right foot, but is possible with the left.

Out Out – "step out, step out" timing is &1

Paddle – "Forward Rock, Turn ¼ and Recover" where the turn is towards the recovering foot, and the timing is 1,2

Push Turn – A sequence of lifting the knee and then pointing the toe, while turning, with timing &1. The amount of turn needs to be clearly specified and will be in the direction of the supporting foot.

Ramble – A series of "Twist both heels in the specified direction, Twist both toes in the same direction" with the necessary weight changes to move along the floor with timing 1,2. A number of ramble actions must be specified

Rocking Chair – "Forward Rock, Recover, Back Rock, Recover" timing is 1,2,3,4

Roll – A travelling and turning series of 3 moves. "Turn ¼ & Forward, Turn ½ and Back, Turn ¼ and Side" where all the turns are in the direction of the first step and with timing 1,2,3. There are many modifiers to change this move in length, direction of turn and direction of travel

Romp – This cluster is different depending on the position of the available foot. If the heel is forward, then the result is the other toe will be backward. It is done with a "Close" in between. So using this as an example a Romp is a: "Close, Point Back" with timing &1.

Run – steps moving forward, for example a Run 4 would be "Forward, Forward, Forward, Forward" with timing 1,2,3,4. If no number is specified a "Run" is only 3 moves

Scissor – "Side, Close, Front" with timing 1&2

Shuffle – A series of "Side, Close, Side, Close" moves with timing 1&2& etc. A number of moves must be specified. It could be considered a "Quick Chasse".

Side Paddle – "Side Rock, Turn ¼ and Recover" where the turn is towards the recovering foot, and the timing is 1,2

Split – "Either toes or heels are twisted apart, then twisted together again" with timing 1,2

Star – "Point Forward, Point Side, Point Back, Point Side" timing is 1,2,3,4. The number of points must be specified.

Stroll – "Diagonal Forward, Lock, Diagonal Forward" with timing 1,2,3

Switch – This cluster is different depending on the position of the available foot. If the foot is pointing to the side, then the result is the other foot pointing to the side. It is done with a "Close" in between. So using this as an example a switch is a: "Close, Point" with timing &1. The start foot could be a toe pointing forward, or be a heel to the diagonal etc.

Swivet – "Twist one toe out and Twist the other heel out, Return the twisted parts to their original place" timing is 1,2

Travelling Applejack – Start as an Applejack, but instead of returning on the next count another applejack action is done in the same direction. Timing is 1&

Triple – A subset of Shuffle with only 3 moves: "Side, Close, Side" with timing 1&2. The direction of the Triple must always be described, as it can also be used to give timing to a cluster such as "Jazz Triple".

Vaudeville – "Side, Front, Side, Diagonal Heel" with timing &1&2

Vee Step – "Diagonal Forward, Side (so feet are apart), Step diagonal back and centre, Close" with timing 1,2,3,4. I have added the "ee" to the V to make it easier to be noticed in documentation.

Vine – A series of "Side, Behind, Side, Front" moves with timing 1,2,3,4. If no number is specified it will be 3 moves starting from the first Side.

Walk – steps moving forward with holds in between, for example a Walk 2 would be "Forward, Hold, Forward, Hold" with timing 1,H,3,H. The number of forward moves must be specified

Weave – "Front, Turn ¼ and Back, Turn ¼ and Side" where the timing is 1,2,3 and the turn (overall ½ turn) is in the same direction as the initial crossing foot.

Modifying Terms

There are "modifying" words that describe changes to the "standard" expectations of a cluster. Potentially there may be more than one modifier to a specific cluster.

Here are some of the common modifying terms:

Action – Often the feature action of a cluster can be replaced with an alternative action. For example a "Coaster Step" can have the last step forward replaced with a point to the side to become a "Coaster Point"

Back – Do the cluster but make it go backward

Behind – Do the cluster but make it go behind

Check – Prepare to change the momentum of the body to the opposite direction. For example "Step Side and Check, Step Side" has the body stepping one way then changing direction and stepping the opposite way

Dual – Use both feet instead of just one

Forward – Do the cluster but make it go forward

Fraction – If a cluster is symmetrical, then it is possible to use a portion of the cluster. For example a ½ Box would be just "Side, Close, Forward, Touch" with timing 1,2,3,4.

Front – Do the cluster but make it go in front.

Interrupted – The steps of an interrupted cluster will stay the same, but the timing of an Interrupted cluster will change. The second beat will become a Hold, and the move that would have been done at that time will be done on the subsequent & beat. So a cluster that has a timing of 1,2,3,4 would now be 1,H&3,4

Late – For clusters that start on an & count usually such as an "Out Out". The cluster will start on a full beat rather than on an & count.

Numeric – Adding a number (2, 3 etc.) after a cluster term means do that number of moves of the cluster. This might mean extending the cluster, or shortening it. If the cluster does not normally need a number, then the actions will all be done on even (non &) counts. For example a Coaster Step is 3 moves with 1&2 timing, whereas a Coaster 3 is the same moves but with 1,2,3 timing.

Open – Do the cluster, but keep the feet apart rather than together

Quick – Done at twice the speed of the standard cluster. For example, if the cluster had the timing 1,2,3,H, then the timing would now be 1&2

Reverse – Do the cluster, but do it in the opposite direction that it usually goes, or turn it the opposite way than it usually turns

Slow – Done at half the speed of the standard cluster. For example if a cluster had the timing 1&2, then the new timing would be 1,2,3,H

Solo – Use one foot instead of the usual two

Sudden – Is started on an & count rather than a full beat

Syncopated – Has an additional & count in second beat of the standard move and the subsequent moves are executed earlier. So a cluster that has a timing of 1,2,3,4 would now be 1,2&3

Travelling – The cluster moves forward (or back if specified Travelling Back) rather than the standard direction which is likely to be stationary

With – Has an additional upper body action associated with it such as Clap, Click, Shimmy etc., or additional actions to change it somehow. An example might be a "Montana Kick with Claps".

Turning Modifiers

Many clusters have turns already included, while some of them can have turns added. Here are some modifiers that can help the dancer determine when to add the turns.

Pre-Turn – Is a turn that is done just before the cluster is commenced. It is described with an '&' as a separator. For example: Turn ¼ Right & Vine Cha

Interior-Turn – Is a turn that is done within the cluster. If the exact position of the turn is needed, then the detailed description of the cluster would need to be given by the instructor. This turn is indicated by the use of the word "Turning", for example "¼ Left Turning Vine Cha". In this case, the turn is likely to be after the second step of the vine and before the triple, making it a forward triple. If there is a natural, comfortable direction of turn for the cluster, then the direction of the turn need not be specified. For example, with a "Jazz Box" starting with the right foot, the natural comfort of the turn is to the Right. A turn to the left is possible, but not very comfortable and rarely asked for. So a ¼ Turning Jazz Box is an acceptable description without specifying the direction of turn.

Post-Turn – Is a turn that is done just after the cluster is completed, or on the last action of the cluster. It is described with an '&' as a separator. For example: Vine Cha & Turn ¼ Right

Turning (without amount or direction) – There are often additional turns involved during the cluster that are not part of the standard definition. If these turns cancel out then neither the amount of turn, nor the direction, need to be specified.

Overturned – turn a bit more than the cluster usually does

Underturned – don't turn as much as the cluster usually does

Rhythm Modifiers

Changing the timing of a cluster is often done by referring to a particular rhythm pattern. The cluster is then modified to take on the rhythm referred to. Line dances are not restricted to using any particular rhythm exclusively, so there may be many different rhythm clusters consecutively. Each rhythm must therefore be unique in its description. I have used the letter "H" to signify a Hold. Be aware that these are the standards I have chosen for line dancing. They may not be technically correct for other forms of dance such as ballroom, but for us it works.

I have also adopted a standard that, if a rhythm modifier is used, then the direction of the extra steps (such as a triple for Cha Cha) must be in the direction of flow of cluster being extended.

Here are the more common rhythm modifiers.

Cha – Timing is 1,2,3&4. Often this will mean adding a triple step instead of the last step of the cluster. So a "Vine Cha" would be "Side, Behind, Side, Close, Side" with timing 1,2,3&4

Foxtrot – Timing is 1,H,3,4. Often this timing is used to modify Waltz specific cluster movements to be used in Common Time music.

Mambo/Triple – Timing is 1&2

Nightclub – Timing is 1,2&

Rumba – Timing is 1,2,3,H

Waltz – Timing is 1,2,3 (rarely used unless modifying a non-waltz movement that usually takes 2 beats to now take 3 beats instead.

Rhythm Based Clusters

Once line dancing started using non country music, choreographers started incorporating non-traditional movements from other dance forms. Initially it was from Cha-Cha, but eventually all the Latin and ballroom rhythms were experimented with. Some of those movements already had definitions in the ballroom environment, but those definitions generally involved the partner aspects of the movement and less accuracy in direction of turn etc. In line dancing we can use those movements but with our own rules and using our own words. Usually they are done in Rumba timing, unless a rhythm modifier is used. Each can be done in the other rhythms by just changing the timing.

The clusters movements "borrowed" from ballroom dancing are:

Cross Rumba – "Cross, Side, Cross, Hold"

Forward Break – "Forward Rock, Recover, Close, Hold"

Forward Rumba – "Forward Rock, Recover, Side, Hold"

Hand to Hand – "Behind Rock, Recover, Side, Hold"

New Yorker – "Cross Rock, Recover, Side, Hold"

Passing Rumba – "Forward Rock, Recover, Back, Hold"

Rumba Turn – "Forward Rock, Turn ½ and Recover, Forward, Hold" where the turn is towards the recovering foot.

Turning Rumba – Forward Rock, Recover and Turn ½, Forward, Hold" where the turn is away from the recovering foot

Other movements whose origins are more specific to dance influences outside of line dancing are:

Basic Cha – The most common definition for a Basic Cha-Cha in line dancing is "Forward Rock, Recover, Back, Close, Back" with timing 1,2,3&4. When I first learned ballroom dancing they said there were three "Basic Cha's", Basic A, Basic B and Basic C. Line dancing cannot survive with that level of ambiguity. It could also realistically be called a Passing Cha.

Charleston – "Point Forward, Back, Point Back, Forward" with timing 1,2,3,4. Adopted from charleston dancing from the early 1920's.

Cuban Break – Same as a New Yorker, but in mambo timing. "Cross Rock, Recover, Side" with timing 1&2. Adopted from mambo.

Diamond Turn – "Forward and Turn 1/8, Side & Turn 1/8, Back" with timing 1,2,3. Adopted from waltz ballroom

Dorothy – The same as a stroll, but in Nightclub timing. "Diagonal Forward, Lock, Diagonal Forward" with timing 1,2&. Adopted from the movies (see "The Wizard of Oz" and Dorothy on the yellow brick road).

Fishtail – "Diagonal Back, Side, Forward, Lock" with timing 1.2.3.4. Adopted from round dancing.

Forward Waltz – "Forward, Close, Close"

Gaucho – A series of: "Forward Rock, Back Rock, Forward Rock, Back Rock" actions with a gradual turn in the specified direction spread over all actions (not just alternating actions like with a paddle). Adopted from tango.

Kick Ball Change – "Kick, Close, Close" with timing 1&2. Adopted from swing dancing.

Lindy – "Side, Close, Side, Back Rock, Recover" with timing 1&2,3,4. Adopted from swing dancing.

Locking Cha – "Diagonal Forward, Lock, Diagonal Forward, Lock, Diagonal Forward" With timing 1,2,3&4

Pas-De-Basque – (Par-De-Bar) "Side, Behind Rock, Recover". This is usually a Waltz movement, but it is utilised in many rhythms just by changing the timing.

Sailor – "Behind, Side Rock, Recover (to the Side)" with timing 1&2. Adopted from the movies and more traditional "Sailor Hornpipe" folk dances.

Sailor Step – A modification of a Sailor: "Behind, Side Rock, Recover Forward" with timing 1&2

Sand Step – "Sugarfoot (2 beats), Front, Hold" with timing 1,2,3,H. Adopted from round dancing.

Serpiente – (Ser-Pee-Ent-Ay) "Front, Side, Behind, Sweep, Behind, Side, Front, Sweep" with timing 1,2,3,4,5,6,7,8. Adopted from tango round dancing.

Sugarfoot – Touch the Toe to the Instep of the other foot, Touch the Heel to the instep of the other foot with the timing 1,2. Adopted from swing dancing.

Tango Draw – "Forward, Side, Draw, Touch" with timing 1,2,3,4. Adopted from tango

Turning Basic Cha – If a Basic Cha has a turn involved in it, then that turn is done during the 3&4 part of the cluster. It will usually be done gradually over the 3 actions causing the feet to trace a "C" shape on the floor, as they go more sideways than back. For a ½ turn with the left foot available it could be described as "Turn ¼ Left and Side, Close, Turn ¼ Left and Forward.

Some choreographers may document it as "Turn ½ Left and Forward, Close, Forward", which does feel slightly different.

Twinkle – "Front, Side, Close" with timing 1,2,3. Adopted from round dancing

Zag – "Diagonal Back, Touch" with timing 1,2. Concept adopted from square dancing

Zig – "Diagonal Forward, Touch" with timing 1,2. Concept adopted from square dancing

Combined Clusters

Just when you thought it couldn't get any more complicated, it can. It is possible to do one cluster with one foot, and another cluster with the other foot. Or do two clusters at a time. Though not common these clusters exist. Here are some examples:

Sugarfoot Ramble – Do a Sugarfoot on one foot, and Ramble with the other

Boogie Run – Do a Run, but Twist the heels in, as you take each step.

Stomping Walk – Do a Walk, but Stomp instead of Step.

Strutting Vine – Do a Vine, but use Toe Struts instead of steps.

Special Case Turn Terminology

For ease of cueing, I have defined the following moves:

Corkscrew – An "Unwind" but a ¾ turn rather than the standard ½ turn.

Full Corkscrew – An "Unwind" but a full turn rather than the standard ½ turn.

I do not consider a ¼ turn Unwind to be an Unwind at all, merely a ¼ turn.

Symmetry Modifiers

Quite often a dance will have symmetry in it. A chunk of choreography is done leading with one foot, then is repeated leading with the other. Leading with the same foot both times is also common. Sometimes it is just a cluster that repeats.

It is a valuable tool to capture that symmetry in the head cues, so that the dancer and teacher can benefit from a low stress chunk.

The symmetry can be indicated using two methods, a leading indicator or a trailing indicator.

"Trailing Indicators" are using the words: Twice, or "3 Times" or "4 Times" after a group of moves or clusters. It is important that there is only one trailing indicator in a chunk. Otherwise it starts getting too mathematically complicated. There should be no further moves in the chunk after the indicator to assist the teaching of the chunk. For example: "Vine 4, Lindy, Twice" would mean "Vine 4, Lindy, Vine 4, Lindy". It would not mean "Vine 4, Lindy, Lindy", the whole chunk must repeat. "Vine 4, Lindy, Twice, Vine 4" is not recommended.

"Leading Indicators" are the use of a number before a single cluster. There can be multiple of these in a chunk, as they relate to the following cluster or move only. For example: "2 New Yorkers", or "4 Heel Closes".

Cluster Families

A specific movement can be part of a group of related movements that form a family. There are too many of these families to fully document, and they are constantly being enlarged as choreographers get more and more creative. I will endeavour to document some of one family to highlight the concept. The family I am documenting is the vine family.

The Vine Family

Vine 4 – As a Vine, but do four moves. So is "Side, Behind, Side, Front". It has the standard timing of 1,2,3,4.

Front Vine – A Front Vine has the same flexibility in length as a Vine, but starts with a Cross in Front. So is "Front, Side, Behind".

Behind Vine – A Behind Vine has the same flexibility in length as a Vine, but starts with a Cross in Behind. So is "Behind, Side, Front".

Vine Front – Starts with a step to the side, but instead of crossing behind on the second move, it crosses in front. So is "Side, Front, Side". If there is a fourth move it would be Behind.

Vine Triple – Same moves as a vine, but has triple timing, so done as 1&2 timing. (I guess it could also be called a Mambo Vine technically).

Slow Vine 4 – Same moves as a Vine 4, but has the timing 1H3H5H7H, so takes 8 beats instead of 4

Quick Vine 4 – Same moves as a Vine 4, but has the timing 1&2&, so takes 2 beats instead of 4

Syncopated Vine 4 – Same moves as a Vine 4, but has the timing 1,2&3, so takes 3 beats instead of 4

Interrupted Vine 4 – Same moves as a Vine 4, but has the timing 1H&3,4, so still takes 4 beats, but there is a little "jump" in the middle.

Turning Vine – Same moves as a Vine, but if starting with the right foot for example, there is a turn ¼ Left before the first side and a turn ¼ Right after the second side.

Nightclub Vine – Same moves as a Vine, but with timing 1,2&

Foxtrot Vine – Same moves as a Vine, but with timing 1H2,3

Vine Cha – First two moves are the same as a Vine, but the third move (the side) is replaced with a "Side Triple". So the timing is 1,2,3&4

Strutting Vine 4 – Side Toe Strut, Behind Toe Strut, Side Toe Strut, Front Toe Strut. Has the Timing of 1,2,3,4,5,6,7,8 and the pattern of a vine 4, but instead of steps there are toe struts.

Front Vine Cha - First two moves are the same as a Front Vine, but the third move (the Behind) is replaced with a "Behind Vine Triple". So the timing is 1,2,3&4

Behind Vine Cha - First two moves are the same as a Behind Vine, but the third move (the Front) is replaced with a "Cross Triple". So the timing is 1,2,3&4. Technically the replacement should be with a Front Vine Triple, but this is not as comfortable as a Cross Triple and less popular, so not worth documenting.

The order of the words in the name, are intended to help you quickly decide what to start with, normal (no word), front or behind, and the number at the end will help you decide how many steps to do.

Other Undefined Moves and Clusters

There are many moves or clusters that I have not included in this book. This has been deliberate and for two main reasons. Firstly I do not want to overwhelm the new dancer or instructor with too much information, there is already enough to scare them here. Secondly, the moves I have not included are rarely used, and therefore I have not created a definition that I am comfortable with. Examples of these are: Anchor Step, Pencil Turn, Knee Knocks, Chicken Shuffles, Moon Walks, Body Waves, Voltas, Hover, Whisk etc.

No doubt over time these will be clarified, maybe in the next edition of this book sometime in the future.

There are also clusters of actions that are crying out to have a good name. Maybe once this book has been digested, a group of like-minded instructors and choreographers can get together to standardise more terms for all of us to use.

For example these need a name:
- Basketball 2, Forward Triple
- Side Rock 2, Forward
- Stamp Forward, Toe Fan, Toe Fan, Toe Fan and Transfer

At least we have a starting point now.

Types of Interruptions

There are lots of different types of interruptions to allow dance phrasing to a piece of music, and each may be only slightly different from the other. But acknowledging these differences actually makes it easier to teach in the long run, rather than calling everything a "Tag" as many people have done till now, and then having to explain what variant is required.

- Addition – Actually a simple variation of a Substitution. An additional move that occurs on a half beat (known as an '&' count) to allow the dancer to get on the correct foot, or to face the right direction for a Restart.
- Bridge – An extra piece of choreography executed between the end of the dance and the beginning of the dance.
- Ending – An additional piece of choreography prior to the conclusion of the music, usually to bring the dancer to the front, sometimes in a dramatic style.
- False Ending – Not really an interruption, but if the music appears to finish, then resumes, it will often cause chaos on the floor as some dancers stop, while others continue.
- Hesitation – A variation of an Insertion. A Hold for a specified period of beats or time and then the dance continues from where it stopped.
- Insertion – An extra piece of choreography that is inserted somewhere inside the sequence and then the sequence resumes where it was interrupted.
- Introduction – An additional piece of choreography done before the dance commences to avoid standing around till the main part of the music and dance begins.
- Jump Start – A variant of Omission. Instead of starting at the beginning of the sequence, the sequence starts part way through.

- Omission – Part of the sequence is missed out and the sequence resumes further in, rather than restarting.
- Option – Like a replacement, but only if the dancer wants to.
- Replacement – An extra piece of choreography that, for a specific sequence, replaces a part of the usual dance. It is usually done to hit some dramatic part of the music that only happens occasionally.
- Restart – A restart occurs when a dance gets part way through a sequence and instead of completing the sequence it stops early and a new sequence is begun.
- Slowing – The dance slows down at a specific place, but the choreography continues. In other words you keep in time with the music.
- Speeding – The dance speeds up at a specific place, but the choreography continues. In other words you keep in time with the music.
- Substitution – An extra piece of choreography that replaces part of the existing sequence and is immediately followed by a restart. This usually occurs when a simple restart would cause the wrong foot to be available.

It is important that the instructor informs the dancers when and where the interruptions will occur, so they can prepare for them. This usually requires counting of sequences. Some examples of Interruptions: Restart after Beat 32 of the 4th Sequence, Do Insertion after Beat 16 of the 6th Sequence and Resume, Do Bridge After the 7th Sequence and Restart.

Counting of sequences is one of the big challenges of a dancer or an instructor. I generally use my fingers to keep track, others use their memories. Whatever works for you, just keep track.

Line Dancer Competencies

For a person to consider they are a competent line dancer (so no longer a beginner) at whatever level, they need to be able to demonstrate the following skills:

- Be a competent Pre-Learner
- Can tell common time music from waltz time music and which is which

- Can dance in time with the music
- Can demonstrate knowledge and understanding of centre of gravity and basic body mechanics
- Can demonstrate knowledge and understanding of action, move and parent cluster terminology
- Can demonstrate knowledge and understanding of Rumba, Cha-Cha, Mambo, Foxtrot and Nightclub timing.
- Can remember complete dances (for a short period of time)
- Can demonstrate knowledge and understanding of the interruptions: Restart, Bridge and Substitution

For a person to be considered a good dancer they should exhibit the following attributes:
- Patience with those that make mistakes around them
- Willingness to move to another spot on the floor if asked
- Is quiet when the teach is being conducted
- Is fluid in their motion on the dance floor
- Doesn't overturn the turns and doesn't over step the actions
- Is reliable in interpreting the instructors commands

Advanced Line Dance Techniques

Line Dancing has been influenced by many other forms of dance. Each of those dance forms has their own sets of rules and standards. But those rules and standards are for the pure form of the original dance form, and are often developed because of standards in the music and environment that those dance forms use. This includes ballroom, tap, clogging, ballet, round, square, Irish, Scottish, folk and many others.

Line dancing is a unique and dynamic dance form with its own challenging environment of mixed rhythms and styles all blended together. It requires its own set of standards and terminology, not an imposition of standards and terminology from other dance forms. We use and experiment with, whatever techniques and terms there are out there. We are also happy to cannibalise and modify those techniques and terms to form something that is workable for the line dance environment, without the need to adhere to any external assumptions that go with them. What we do in line dancing is not wrong, it's just different, and it's ours.

Many descriptions have been simplified to keep dance sheets sufficiently compact to fit onto a single page. How a dance sheet describes a collection of moves may not completely describe the way that they may actually be executed in reality. Much of the style and body mechanics of the clusters are not written down. They are learned by experience, and rarely transferred from teacher to student. Often this is because the teacher is not aware that they are happening, even though they may be doing the style themselves.

Ballroom Foot Positions

The ballet and ballroom community have documented the various foot positions and given those positions names such as "First Position", "Second Position" etc. Though I am sure it is technically important in other dance forms, I have found limited need to teach this information in the general social line dance environment.

However, moving forward with the onslaught of new style of dances now coming through line dancing, it may be a good idea to start recognising, if only some, the foot positions/techniques of these other styles. I have found ballroom descriptions to be the closest to what we use, more than ballet.

The ballroom definitions of foot positions are as follows:
- First Position – Feet together, side by side. The toes may be turned out
- Second Position – Feet shoulder width apart, side by side. The toes may be turned out
- Third Position – Feet together, but with the heel to the instep and that foot will be at a slight angle to the other foot
- Extended Third Position – Feet apart, but with the heel closer to the instep and that foot will be at a slight angle to the other foot

FOR THE DANCERS

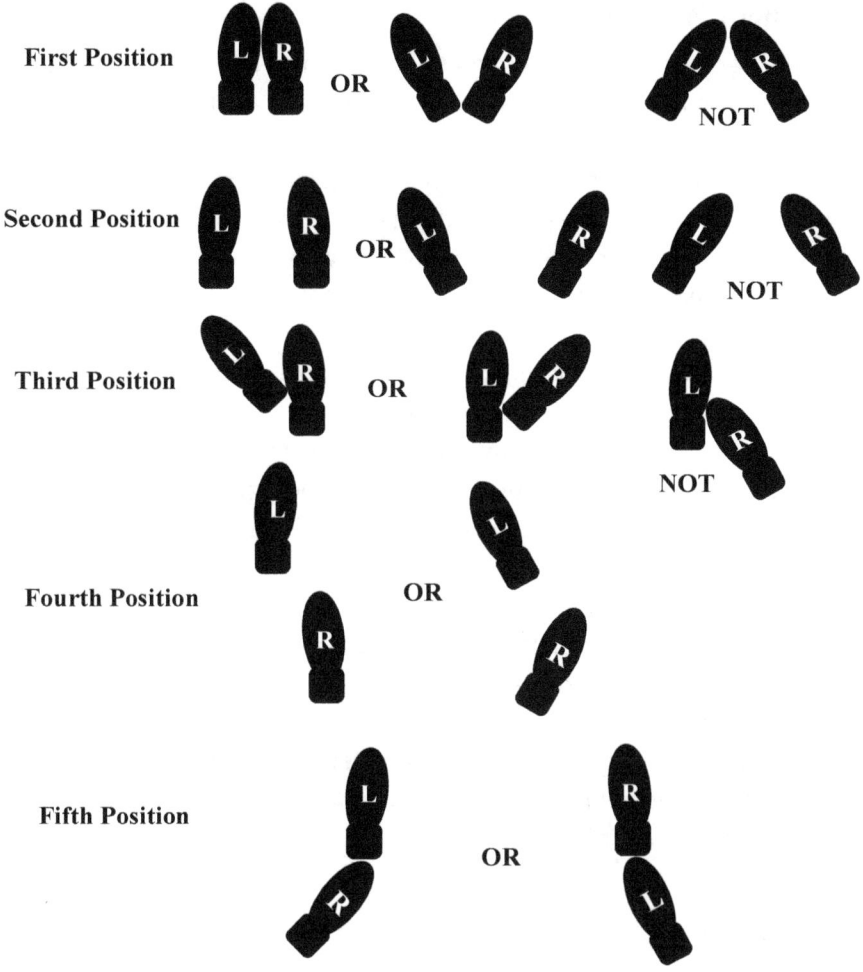

- Fourth Position – Feet apart with one foot forward of the other, which is what you do when walking down the street. The toes may be turned out (though you probably wouldn't walk that way down the street)

- Fifth Position – Feet together with one foot in front of the other, toe to heel (either foot in front) and the trailing foot has the heel turned behind

- Extended Fifth Position – Feet apart with one foot directly in front so the heel is in front of the toe and the trailing foot has the heel turned behind

Contra Body Movement

Many dancers turn their shoulders to follow their hips when executing a movement like a "vine". It makes the dancing feel flowing and nice. There is a downside however. It can also cause the dancer to lose orientation easily. Ideally when executing travelling crossing steps, the hips will turn for comfort, but the shoulders should remain in the correct facing direction. This is called Contra Body Movement (CBM), where the hips and shoulders are turned different ways.

Contra Body Movement happens when you are walking along, allowing the natural swing of your arms with your stride. When you step forward with your left foot, your right arm goes forward in a very natural balancing movement. This will cause your hips to be turned right and your shoulders to be turned left. This is also the action you use for many preparations into the turns in dancing.

Contra Body Movement Position (CBMP) is a term that refers to the position you are in if you make a contra body movement and freeze. You can simply stand and put one foot slightly across in front of the other foot, and it will look like you have used CBM but actually you have not moved the body. You have simply placed your foot towards the contra side of the body, or so to say you have "placed it in CBMP."

Heel and Toe Leads

If shoulder turning or losing balance on crossing steps is a problem, an effective technique is to use a "heel lead" when doing the crossing action in front and a "toe lead" when crossing in behind. This means turning the moving foot at the ankle, so the leading part of the foot is the heel (or toe) rather than a straight foot. This will cause the hips to remain in the forward direction.

It also gives the body an angled foot to stand on which makes a lot of difference when trying to keep your balance. This is a technique used heavily in ballet and Latin American ballroom.

Using a heel lead into an action requiring a turn, such as a ¼ turning jazz box will assist in getting the correct turn.

Cuban Motion

As Latin ballroom dancing started integrating into line dancing, so too did some of the Latin dance styling. Generally this is optional styling, but is sometimes mentioned on the dance sheets.

Cuban motion (sometimes called Cuban hips) is characterised by the rhythmic swaying of the hips, caused by the bending and straightening of the knees. It is a style of movement developed in Latin American dances, such as mambo, salsa, rumba and cha-cha. As a knee bends, the same hip drops. As a knee straightens, the same hip lifts. There is no hip rotation in Cuban motion, it is all lifting and dropping of the hips. There is also an associated sideways shifting of the ribcage on sideways actions.

Here is a technique for teaching yourself Cuban hip motion, reproduced from Joe Baker from "The Dance Store". It uses forward and back mambo steps as the basis for the teach. You can consult their videos for further clarification.

Step 1—Loosen Up by Bending and Straightening the Knees

Begin by standing in place with your feet together and alternately bending and straightening your left and right knees. As a knee bends allow the same hip to drop.

Step 2—Add Stepping Action to the Bending Action

Next, begin stepping in place and continue the alternate bending and straightening action. Try to make complete weight changes with each step. Remember; as a knee bends allow the same hip to drop.

Step 3—Make Distinct Steps Using Ball-Flat Footwork

The correct footwork is ball-flat for all steps. All steps are taken to the inside edge of the ball of the foot. The ball of the foot hits the floor first, and then you lower to the flat of the foot. All steps should be distinct. A mistake is to shuffle the feet. Again, try to make complete weight changes with each step.

Step 4—Add Contra-Body Action

Keep your hands above your waist and add contra-body upper body action to the stepping and bending action. So when the left foot goes forward, the right arm goes forward.

Step 5—Isolate the Rib Cage

In Latin dancing, steps to the side entail a natural lead of the rib cage. First loosen up the rib cage. Stand in place, hold your lower body still and move your rib cage alternately from left to right. Be careful not to tilt your upper body.

On steps to the side, the ribcage will lead. Thus as the left foot steps out to the left, the rib cage slides over to the left. Don't forget that the left hip will drop as the left knee bends in preparation for stepping to the left. Again, be careful not to tilt your upper body.

Step 6—Put it all together

With your feet together, step in place, making distinct steps, using the ball-flat footwork. The stepping action should be accompanied by the alternate bending and straightening of the knees. Remember, as a knee bends, the same hip drops. Conversely, as a knee straightens, the same hip rises. This is why the steps feel like you are pushing into the floor. Incorporate the contra-body upper body action. Be sure to keep your hands above your waist. Now let's go from stepping in place to making a basic mambo step pattern. The step timing is quick quick slow, quick quick slow. The small step to the side should entail a natural rib cage lead.

Step 7—The Most Important: Practice

At first, you will need to think about the actions and the steps. You might feel awkward. As you practice, everything will begin to feel natural and to look natural. Review and practice every day or as often as possible until the actions become as natural and as automatic as tying a shoe.

Waltz Technique

To execute proper waltz technique, all waltz forward steps should be a heel forward. It is what gives the waltz its true 'rise and fall' action. Generally it is; "Heel, toe, toe lower" or "down, down up, down". The following graph (copied with permission from BallroomGuide.com) shows where you should be in your rise and fall at any point in a waltz measure.

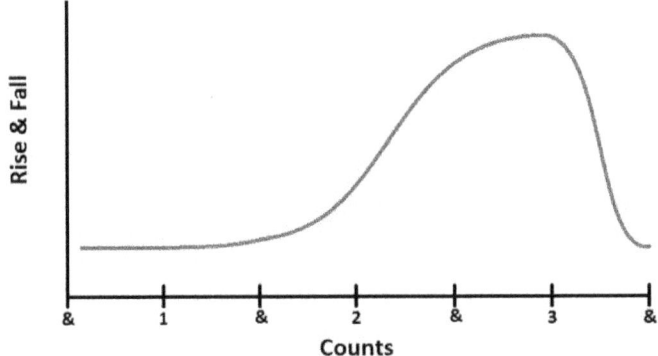

So the first step should be reasonably flat, the second should commence the rise. The third step should complete the rise, and then there is a fall before the next first step is commenced. This rise is partly generated because, as you bring your feet together from a position with feet apart, you will gain height. Waltz technique assumes that the standard pattern of steps are "forward, forward, close", or "forward, side close", so the feet don't come together until the third beat.

Many choreographers in line dancing do not understand this, and often describe a "forward, close, close" sequence, which would shift the rise to the second beat rather than the third if the ballroom technique is followed.

This makes it difficult, but not impossible, to properly execute correct waltz technique.

In this circumstance, assuming starting on the left foot: step left foot down and forward going from heel to toe, bending the right knee slightly touch the right toe alongside the first foot changing weight to the ball of the right foot rising up as you straighten the right knee, close the left toe alongside right toe and then lower the left heel and bend the right knee in preparation for the next step forward with the right foot.

This is important in general because, if we are going to do waltzing in line dancing, it should be at least the same action as the dance form that inspired it. This is especially important if you are a competition dancer.

Prepping for a Turn or Balance

Usually a dance will require a turn after a step at some stage. Sometimes those turns feel awkward because they do not feel part of the flow of the dance. Often the choreographer does not build comfort in their definitions on the dance sheet. There are a number of techniques called "prepping" (short for preparation) that will assist in making these turns more comfortable.

- Foot Prepping – If a dance instructs you to step to the side and turn in that direction, by turning the foot in the required direction before stepping, this will assist in making the turn comfortable. It will create a slight twist of the leg initially, but as the weight is transferred to that foot, it will cause the shoulders to turn, thereby assisting in making the turn. If you are competition dancing, this is changing the dance, so shouldn't be done in that situation.

- Lean Prepping – When pointing a toe out to the side with no weight bearing, it is important to lean a little in the opposite direction to counterbalance the weight of the leg. If you don't do this, you will tend to put more weight on the pointed foot than is intended. This is especially an issue when coming out of a turn, such as a turn and step, then point.

- Shoulder Prepping – When doing a large turn on the spot from a stationary position (such as in a Monterey), that turn may feel hard to start. If you slightly twist the shoulders away from the intended turn on the previous move, the resultant untwisting action will assist in getting the desired turn started.

- Under-turn Prepping - If coming out of a turn into a vine, the turn of the shoulders can force the feet to cross in front rather than behind. If you don't complete the turn till the next step, then the shoulders will not influence the feet as much.

Modifications for Comfort and Style

Once you start adding individual moves together to create clusters, there are small modifications that you make to the component parts to make the overall cluster more comfortable or more stylish to watch and execute. Here are some examples.

- When doing a "forward triple", the standard description is "Forward / Close, Forward". However the Close is not really executed as a Close. The second step is often done in third position rather than first position. The toes definitely do not come alongside each other before the third step is commenced. This is especially the case if the triple is being executed at high speed.
- When doing a "cross triple", the standard description is "Cross / Side, Cross", however the three steps are really done in fifth position or extended fifth position, with the left heel turned right and the right heel turned left as you cross across with the left foot
- When doing a Coaster Step, the upper body is leaned forward during the first "Back / Close" moves to make the third "Forward" move to be more comfortable.
- When doing the first move of a Monterey Turn, the upper body is turned away in contra body motion and the heel of the pointed foot is often twisted out and the same knee is rotated slightly down. This creates a torsion effect that allows the turn to be done comfortably and with style on the second count.
- When doing the first move of a New Yorker with the left foot, the feet are actually in an extended fifth position, with the left heel turned right and the right heel turned left as you rock across with the left foot. This reduces the amount of turn of the shoulders.
- When doing a Charleston, the upper body will twist contra body to the pointed toe with the both arms swinging from side to side.
- When doing a Basketball/Pivot, slightly cross the rocking foot in front of the stationary foot. This will allow the feet to be comfortable aligned after the turn is complete. If you don't do this the legs will end up slightly crossed and the shoulders may not fully turn, leading to potential issues with the aligning to the wall for the next move.

- When doing a Cross, followed by an Unwind, try wrapping the crossing leg around the supporting leg before placing the foot. As you unwind, this will give you a more balanced foot position and the feet will be slightly apart when you finish the Unwind. This is especially important for unwinds of greater than a half turn.

FOR THE COACH

If a group of line dancers are going to do a public presentation of line dancing, they will need to select a "Coach" to coordinate the overall style of the presentation. This should be a person respected by the team. It need not be a dancer, but should be someone who knows line dancing and what looks good.

I have prepared dancers for television, movie and stage-show events over the last twenty years. Each event has its own requirements, no two are the same. We have even danced at funerals for some of the fanatics that have passed away over the years.

If someone has asked you to perform at an event, other than a funeral, you should receive some compensation for your efforts. It may be just petrol money, but there should be some payment involved. If you do it for free, you tend to be treated less favourably than other performers that are being paid. The customer is more likely to want to get value for money, so will be less likely to bump you for another performer.

If you perform for free, word will get out, and you will get inundated with requests from organisations that need fillers for some small gathering somewhere. If you do it for one, you will be expected to do it for their friends, then their friends of friends, and so on.

You should also ensure that your team is operating with a valid and current public liability insurance policy, and that the event you are performing at also has a current public liability policy. Unlike a class environment, there are many unknown factors associated with a performance that may cause an accident and subsequent injury. You do not want to be liable for team members, or general public member's medical costs.

Any sound equipment you use should be electrically tested. Sometimes there will be government or venue restrictions requiring the equipment to be tested and tagged to verify that it is safe to use, before you will be allowed to plug it in to the venues power supply.

Performance Line Dancing

Preparing a team of dancers for a performance is a challenging task. Not only do you need to coordinate the execution of the actions, but positioning, spacing and above all smiling are all important.

The selection of the choreography is important. When choosing a dance you should consider the upper body movement of the dance. If it is all steppy or twisty actions, then the audience behind the first couple of rows will not be able to see any movement. Add claps, slaps and clicks to liven up the action. Not all "really great" dances are good to watch from a spectator's perspective.

It is professional to plan and execute an entry and an exit for the presentation, rather than just wandering on and off the dance floor.

The entrance should allow each of the dancers to be presented to the audience; they all are providing the entertainment. Make the back row parade in first, then the next, and so on till all the performers are on the floor. Ensure the stronger dancers are on the ends and especially the corners. If there is a back and a front to the audience, then ideally, the taller ones should be near the back. Traditionally, men should be at the back or sides, to present the ladies at all times.

The formation of the dancers will depend on how many you have in the presentation. How many you can use will depend on the space available and the number of capable dancers available. You should have a space of at least six metres by six metres for a team of nine or so dancers.

Some of the possible neat formations are in the following figure.

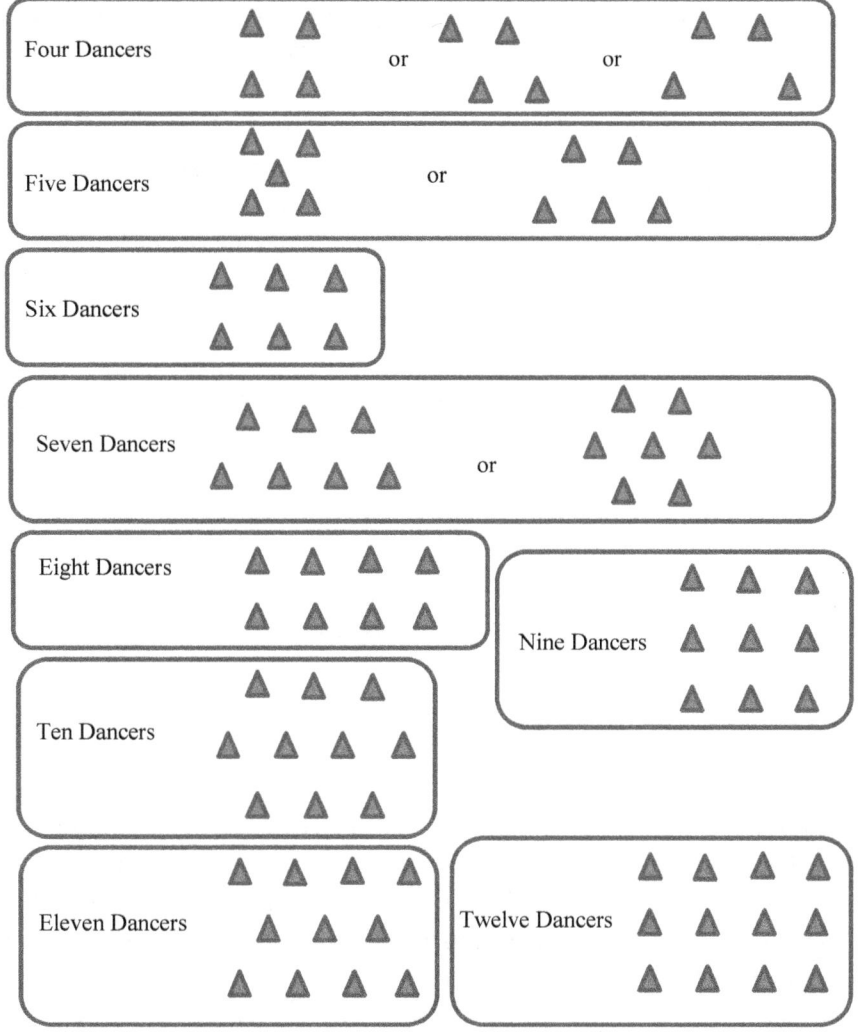

When there are uneven numbers of dancers in rows, then the dancers behind should be visible in the gaps between the front dancers. This takes practice, as the dancers will naturally fall into lines and destroy the pattern. Similarly if there are dancers out on the end by themselves, they will tend to drift into line with others. These people need to be reliable and competent dancers.

The spacing of the dancers is important. It must be even throughout the formation. The size of the spacing may be influenced by the available space at the venue. If not, then using elbows touching for a tight formation, or fingertips touching for a spread formation is an effective way to regulate the spacing. Make sure you do it in both the sideways, and the forward and back directions.

If using hats, put one finger above the eyebrows and pull down on the brim. This makes the hats uniformly straight and even over the group. Look out at the audience as a whole with heads up and faces relaxed. Try to avoid "deer in headlights" panic looks or facial distortions when a mistake is made. No one might know a mistake has been made unless your facial expressions give you away.

Most of all whatever the performance, the hardest thing to get the performers to do is SMILE. Line dancers always look so sour, because they are concentrating. Smiling can take practice, but is very important if you want people to think you are actually enjoying yourselves.

It is important to understand the purpose of the performance to ensure the correct style of presentation is prepared. There are two main types of presentation, a "Demonstration" and a "Floorshow".

Demonstration Line Dancing

A Demonstration is designed to encourage the spectators to think that they would be capable of doing what is being demonstrated. It is a great vehicle for recruiting people into line dancing. There generally should be an opportunity to teach a simple dance to the spectators to reinforce both the pleasure and the achievability of the activity.

It is at these demonstrations that you should highlight the diversity of the music we use and the variety of the people we have doing the activity. Perfection should not be important, smiling and laughter should be encouraged. Degree of dance difficulty should be kept very low. Music should be lively and happy, with no interruptions unless they are very simple and obvious.

When at a class, it is important for the Coach to step back and watch each dance as a spectator. A dance might feel wonderful to do, but may be really boring to watch. Other dancers that might feel tedious to a dancer might look really impressive to a spectator. This will help you select a presentation that will best highlight line dancing.

Floorshow Line Dancing

A floorshow is far more challenging to prepare for. Often the floorshow team is hired to do the presentation, and the paying customer will have an idea of what they want for their money. Quite often they will dictate the style of the music and the length of the presentation. It will often be associated with a theme they have for the function. Usually their expectation is very country and very "Yee Haah". This is our roots and this is what the audience expects. We can try to "educate" the audience, but they are the customer, so should be listened to if you want any follow up bookings, or even to be paid for the current performance.

If working from a stage, the presentation may need to be structured to face mainly in one direction. The selection of the choreography used is very important. It must not travel too far, as falling off the stage is not a good idea.

It is unlikely that doing one specific piece of choreography will keep the attention of the audience for a full song. Often it is wise to prepare a "combo". A Combo is two or more dances that can be spliced together. Do four sequences of one dance, then smoothly transition to another dance for four more sequences, then return to the first dance (or a third dance), for the rest of the song. Do not just alternate the dances, as it will just look like one long dance being repeated.

The handwork needs to be practiced and perfected, to be of even height and timing. The hands when not being used to clap or click need to be placed in a planned place for all dancers. This may be in belt, at sides or behind back. Even the position of the fingers should be standardised rather than some clenched and others splayed.

If there is hat or skirt work involved, then the men's arms should roughly mimic the ladies skirt work, or go to a neutral position.

The selection of the music for the presentation should be appropriate to the theme of the event. Some customers will want to know the playlist before the event so they can check it for appropriateness of lyrics. This is their prerogative, they are hiring you.

The selection of costumes is out of the scope of this book, but it often helps to have more than one costume, and to make it as quick change as possible using vests or quick fit accessories.

Competition Line Dancing

Competition line dancing has become a popular extension of the line dance industry. The style and precision of ballroom dancing has become part of the line dance style at this level of performance.

Arm-work, hat-work and skirt-work are usually part of the styling.

In solo line dance competition a very careful knowledge of the original dance sheet is critical, and any issues with the sheet should be immediately clarified before rehearsals begin. You cannot use any online video to confirm details, even if it is the choreographer in the video. Confirmation can only come from the competition organisers. The competition may provide their sheet to be used, and this sheet must be the one followed.

Each competition's rules can change slightly from year to year, and each governing organisation's rules can also change from event to event. This tends to happen for currency and relevance reasons and is not such a bad thing. You must read and re read the rules thoroughly each time, so as to not disadvantage yourself. Do not assume things from previous events without verifying the facts.

FOR THE INSTRUCTOR

Line dance teaching is developing into a style I call "Voice Over Dance". Other dance forms that fit this category are square dancing, round dancing and clogging.

"Voice Over Dance" is a style of dance done to music, but with an overlay of voice commands. For these other dance forms such as square dancing, the voice is an essential part of the dance form, and it cannot be performed without it. This is because the dance form is so complex as to need commands to supplement the memory, or is freestyle in nature, so the dancer has no prior knowledge of the intended choreography.

Line dancing is not yet at the point that the verbal commands are essential through the whole dance. They are important in teaching, and in reminding the dancer of any interruptions or changes to the regular structure of the patterns. For this reason, understanding the voice over music skills is still important.

It is also important to understand about the other parts of your product, such as your venue, your staff, your music, and of course your own personal well-being and presentation skills.

Venues

Selecting the right venue to conduct your class is very important. There are many factors to consider. Be aware that generally line dancers don't drink alcohol when dancing, they need to concentrate. So if you are in a venue that serves alcohol and is expecting to be patronised, you may not be popular in the long run. Many line dance classes have been closed because of this.

Flooring

The dance floor should preferably be a sprung wooden floor. It is important that there is some "give" in the floor to reduce the shock on the dancer's legs when performing the actions. Because of the various turns, using a carpeted floor is quite dangerous and is likely to cause twisting injuries to knees, ankles and hips. Using a concrete floor without any padding is also dangerous and will cause jarring injuries over time. Parquetry or linoleum over concrete is tolerable though not ideal.

There are various types of wood used for floors, and various ways that owners use to keep them in good condition. Though this is not really part of the instructor's job, it is worthwhile knowledge.

Most floors should be made of hard wood, as it resists being worn down. To keep it clean it is usually surfaced or treated in some way. The wood is either: polished, oiled or coated. These different surfaces cope differently with the wear of dancers spinning and turning. Many classes have been denied use of a hall because they "damage" the floor. Often dancer's shoes create a white powder where they are dancing.

This is because the cleaners use an inferior polish product that breaks down easily. Using the correct polish should stop this from happening. Some polishes also react badly to humidity, causing them to become excessively grippy which could lead to wrenching injuries on the joints.

Stage

It is often good to have a stage to elevate the instructor, so that the dances at the back have a better chance of seeing them. Only use the stage if you are comfortable you won't walk off it during teaching. It needs to be wide enough to dance on and also fit your sound equipment. Otherwise just use it as a table and teach from in front of it. The dance surface on the stage is almost as important to you as the main dance floor. If the stage is carpeted, you may cause yourself injuries over a period of time.

Acoustics

Having bad acoustics in your venue is a class killer. Assuming that you have some control over the venue, or changing venues is not an option, then there are things that can be done to improve acoustics. The general problem is too much echo. Any noise is bounced back off the walls, ceiling and floor, sometimes multiple times, creating a muddled or ringing sound. Sometimes this sound is partially absorbed by the dancers once the room is full. If there are not a lot of dancers, then there is still a problem.

There are ways to stop the reflection of the sound. You can hang curtains on the bare walls, or over the windows. These curtains will absorb the sound very effectively. There are also sound absorbing materials such as acoustic tiles with minute holes in them, or spray on material made of fibres which can be then painted over, which is often used on ceilings.

If you can't actually change the venue, then you may need to change how you set up your sound equipment. Try changing your treble and bass settings on your amplifier to reduce the high or low frequencies that are being bounced. Point your speaker into a corner, rather than directly at a wall, so you don't get an immediate bounce back. You may even try setting your speakers up in a corner or maybe pointing at the front. Try all sorts of variations to see if you can reduce the effect of the echo.

Ventilation

Ventilation and cooling is also very important. Line dancing can be quite energetic and, if there is no way of cooling the body or getting fresh oxygen into the venue, then the customers will not return. Often fans are preferable over evaporative air-conditioning, as the air conditioning may cause the floor to get sticky in the humidity. Depending on the environment, heating may also be important to at least take the chill off the venue before the class. Refrigerative air conditioning will keep the temperature down, but may not provide sufficient air flow, so may need to be supplemented with fans.

Insurance

It is important to have a current "Public Liability" insurance policy when conducting classes. Your venue should also have one to cover any venue related issues such as breakages or falls outside. The venue is not liable for injuries related to incorrect or dangerous instructions or actions by the instructor. That is the instructor's responsibility, unless the instructor is being hired by the venue, and that arrangement is covered in the venue's insurance policy.

The instructor cannot control decisions made by the dancers, but if the instructor asks the dancer to do something that is dangerous, then it is the instructor that may be found liable and therefor their insurance policy that is activated.

It is a duty of care for the instructor to give low impact alternatives for jumps, twists or turns, if they are aware of health issues with individual dancers. If the dancer then decides to do the higher impact version, then that was the dancer's choice and the instructor is unlikely to be found liable should an injury occur.

The instructor should check the dance surface before conducting the class for anything that could cause injury, such as raised nails, chewing gum or spilt liquids.

Venue Hiring Conditions

Each venue will have its own set of conditions that you as a hirer will be required to agree to. These may include length of agreement, cost of hiring, noise restrictions and probably many others. There are a few tips that I can provide that may reduce your future issues.

Have a written agreement with the venue before the class is created. I have known of venues that have changed hiring conditions soon after a successful class gets started. They try to maximise their returns, after the instructor has done the hard work in gathering the customers and promoting the class.

Decide on a policy regarding public holidays and school holidays. Some venues are unavailable during school holidays, even if you wish to run your classes, so check beforehand.

Decide on a hot weather policy if the venue is not air conditioned. This may be as simple as saying "the class goes on no matter what".

Some venues will require you to pay for the venue hire, even if you do not use the venue for whatever reason. Others will be more accommodating. This is important if you have to cancel a class because of low attendance, health issues, bad weather or power outages. Many venues require you to pay for the rent in advance.

Some venues will set a per-head charge, rather than a time or day based charge. In this case, they will probably require you to do some book keeping to validate your statistics. This is great if you have variable or low numbers, but less beneficial if you have consistently large numbers. It does give the venue incentive to promote your class, as they also benefit.

It is wise to negotiate an expiring contract some time before the expiration date. Often a greedy venue will change the terms of the new agreement, giving you little time to negotiate an alternative venue or alternative terms.

Clarify who "owns" the class as part of any contract. Some venues hire instructors to conduct classes that are owned by the venue operators. In this condition, they are in their rights to replace the instructor with another if they choose to do so. No-one owns the customers however.

Know what you can and cannot do with the surface of the floor. Some floors are sticky and need to be powdered; some are too fast and need to be soaped. Your venue may have restrictions on what you are allowed to put on the floor to assist your dancing.

Ensure there is a park you can have for your vehicle to enable easy delivery of any equipment you have to carry. Some venues may have a house public address system that you can use for your classes. Make sure you have permission to do so, and understand any issues that may arise should it not work as planned. Have a backup plan in these circumstances.

Some venues will allow access to kitchen facilities for tea and coffee etc., while others may charge an additional fee to access these facilities should you need them.

Clarify who is responsible for cleaning the hall, and who is responsible for cleaning the toilets, including the provision of toilet paper, soap and towels.

Know your Dancers and Yourself

A good instructor will understand what motivates their students to come to class. Each dancer will be motivated by different things. It is a challenge to keep all the dancers motivated and enthused. Each instructor is also motivated by different things. You need to understand as an instructor what decisions you make for you, and what decisions you make for the dancers. When you make these decisions you need to then be comfortable with the likely outcome.

One characteristic you will need to develop early on in your instructor development is a "thick skin". People will hassle you about every imaginable thing under the sun as soon as you pick up a microphone. They will try to influence you to do things the way they want it. They will gossip and tell stories when you are not there. It is all part of the joys of being in the public eye. There is always someone who thinks they know better. It's not going away, so just get used to it and do your own thing. The customer is not always right; they just need to think that they are.

FOR THE INSTRUCTOR

What sort of Instructor do you want to be?

Each person has their own style and personality. This personality will come out naturally when you are teaching, and to some degree will determine the type of customers you will attract. Some of the styles of instructor I have come across are:

- Carefree – Don't really mind what people think or want, does their own thing.
- Chatterbox – Says lots, but not much content. Sometimes said to have "Verbal Diarrhoea".
- Fun/Comic – Lots of joking around without taking anything very seriously.
- Pedantic – Everything is accurate and specific, and that is what they would like from their dancers.
- Racey – Everything is fast and furious. The teaching, the dance, the music.

What sort of customers do you want?

Here are some types of class choices:

- If you only cater for the dancers that are motivated by the challenge of the choreography, then you will develop into a class for high end dancers and therefor a small elite group of people.
- If you only cater for the dancers that are motivated by the social contact with other people then you will end up running a tea party for a lot of people with occasional dancing.
- If you only run classes at night, you will cater for the younger and working people, but the seniors often won't go out at night.
- If you only run classes in the day, then you won't cater for the working people or the children at school.
- If you run classes targeted at younger people, you will be always looking for replacement dancers, as the young ones change interest, change boyfriends, get married, or have babies.
- If you run classes targeted at seniors, you will suffer from seasonal attendance waves as the seniors join the "snowbird" or "grey-nomad" fraternity and travel interstate or go cruising chasing the warmth for months on end.

If you try to cater for all these conflicting motivations then no one will be completely happy. All you can do is what you think is right, and hope you make the right decisions for you.

Remember, if you stretch the ability of a large class with difficult dances, when many of them don't want to stretch, then you will no longer have a large class. They will go somewhere else or worse for you, start a competing class of their own.

What is a Beginner?

A beginner is someone who has not yet achieved all of the line dancer competencies. This may take six months or more to accomplish, but each person learns at their own speed. Even when they have achieved all the competencies, this makes them an adequate dancer, not necessarily a good one.

Some people move on too soon. Others move on too late, and get bored at the beginners class, which usually disrupts the class. A lot depends on what options are available to them in the area that they live.

If you cannot provide what is needed to a specific individual, then it is professional to pass them to a class that is more suitable, rather than losing them to line dancing all together (if one exists).

What if someone can't do the simplest of dances?

There are some people that will never get it. Sometimes you just have to make that decision and move on. Sometimes it might be a physical issue, sometimes a mental issue. Sometimes it just isn't going to work. In this circumstance, occasionally high degrees of perseverance will pay off, but the potential dancer needs to be exceptionally motivated and the teacher very patient. This goes for all fields of endeavour, not just dancing.

I'm not a Beginner, I'm a Dancer!

Many people assume that, if they have done some sort of dancing before, then it will be easy to pick up line dancing. Ballroom dancers, rock 'n' rollers, tap dancers, cloggers; they all make that assumption. An expert lawn tennis player will not make an expert table tennis player without any lessons. It's the same issue.

Even if you have line danced elsewhere, each class and each teacher will have its own style and selection of material, which will take a while to adjust to. Line dancing looks so easy, when it's done by people that know what they are doing. But it takes time to learn the moves, terminology and body mechanics.

I can't get it! Am I stupid?

Some people have a very high opinion of their abilities. I have found that it takes, on average, about seven classes before the dancer starts to train their muscles and brains to operate automatically. It is wonderful to witness that "light bulb" moment, when they get their first dance all the way through. Encourage them to persevere, it is worth it.

If a beginner is able to go to multiple beginners classes a week, it vastly shortens their learning time. Each teacher teaches differently, and sometimes a different instructor will get the message across better for different types of dancers. Often however this is not an option due to travel time and availability of classes.

Have you met these People?

While running classes, I have noticed there are individuals that dance that have unique characteristics. Wouldn't the world be boring, if we were all alike? I have captured some pet names for some of these characters.

Angel – An Angel is an experienced dancer who attends an easy level class to assist the instructor by giving the newer dancers someone to follow in times of panic or doubt. These people are so helpful in keeping the class flowing and in keeping teaches shorter than might otherwise be needed.

Bragger – A dancer who lets you know they dance at a higher level.

Clown – Most classes, if you are lucky, will have a class clown. This is someone who deliberately acts up to get attention. They are often a good person for the instructor to joke around with, without offending someone else that you don't know how to deal with. It is important that you have a private discussion with that person to ensure they are happy to be treated as a clown without getting offended. Sometimes it is a persona they put on to hide insecurity and you may unwittingly upset them and drive them away.

Counter – A dancer that always needs the numbers, even if it is just 1,2,3,4,5,6,7,8.

Creative – A Dancer who makes up steps, when they have forgotten what they are supposed to do, often with disastrous or entertaining consequences.

Devil – A Devil is an experienced dancer who, even though they are capable, refuse to get on the floor, to assist in a teach, or walk through, of a dance. These people may have a good reason, but it makes the teach take much longer than might otherwise be the case with them on the floor.

Tipsy – A Dancer who appears to lurch all over the place in a drunken manner while dancing, even without the help of alcohol.

Echo – A dancer who verbalises everything you say a split second after you say it.

Economist – A dancer that wants value for money, so no breaks, just dance. Don't think of finishing a class early if they are around.

Gossip – A person who loves passing on pieces of information from other classes or teachers.

Guilty – A dancer who cannot help giving themselves away; when they make a mistake. This is often by saying a word (sometimes rude), a giggle, or a sigh. Sometimes it will be a tell-tale facial expression, a flap of the arms, or a tongue poked out of the side of the mouth. It is instinctive, and entertaining.

Hottie – A dancer who always wants the fans on, even if the temperature is near zero.

Hummer – A dancer who hums or sings along to the music as they dance.

Hyper – A Hyperactive dancer that doesn't want to stop, just keep dancing. They will get faster and faster if you let them.

Icicle – A dancer who always wants the heaters on, even in summer.

Indecisive – A dancer who plans to take a turn out, forgets, or changes their mind half way through, with entertaining consequences.

Intimidator – What they want they get, or else.

Latecomer – A dancer that is always late to class, no matter what.

Magnet – Wherever you are, so are they. You walk into the hall and they approach you. You walk off the stage, there they are.

Mouse – A timid or fragile dancer who doesn't want to be noticed or picked on. They may suffer anxiety, and it is best to leave them to their own devices rather than trying to help them. You may not realise this till too late however.

Name Dropper – A Name Dropper is a dancer who knows everyone and everything, and make sure that you know they know, constantly.

Petrol Head – A Petrol Head is a dancer that is always asking for the fastest, hardest and most turning dances possible.

Pretender – A dancer who pretends they don't know a dance, and then miraculously are able to do it with no walk through.

Princess – A Princess is a dancer whose main focus is about being seen with the "in fashion dancers", rather than with the general dancer population. They dance to impress others, rather than for personal enjoyment.

Racketeer – A dancer who loves to whoop and holler at every opportunity. They add atmosphere to a class or demonstration, but occasionally need to be toned down when people are concentrating.

Searcher – A Dancer that is always scanning around looking for someone to watch and follow. They should be encouraged to dance for themselves, rather than trusting others.

Show Pony – A Show Pony is a dancer who persists in adding spins and turns into dances, often even in the walk throughs. Quite often they are incapable of doing the dance "vanilla" because of their habit.

Shusher – A dancer who is always asking for the music to be turned down. Often they will stand right in front of the speaker, but won't move to another spot on the dance floor.

Slacker – A dancer who doesn't care about execution or correctness. Just does the minimum to get through the dance and move on. They don't want to be told, but usually think they are doing it right.

Slouch – A dancer who always leans over and watches their own feet. This causes bad posture and neck issues and they might not know they are doing it.

Smart Ass – Someone who can and does, dance a dance backwards.

Snob – A dancer who won't dance a dance because it is too easy for them, or not written by one of the renowned choreographers.

Sponge – A dancer who absorbs and internalises everything you say, always wanting more and more knowledge, and wants to do it "right". Often they will become a potential relief or trainee instructor. Could also be called an "Oliver" from the book/movie, always wanting MOOORE.

Vampire – They suck you dry of happy thoughts. If you weren't depressed before speaking to them, you are now.

Selecting the Dance Choreography to Teach

One of the challenges of being an instructor is to appropriately select the dances to be taught to the class. Do you pick dances that you want to do and disregard what the customers might like? Do you pick dances that you think the customers might like, and disregard your personal taste and desires?

This may depend on whether you are teaching as a career to make money, or teaching as a hobby for your own self-gratification. Whichever you choose, it is probably best to make it clear in your publicity, so you don't mislead the customers.

Getting the Level Right

If it takes longer than thirty minutes to teach a dance to a group of dancers, whatever their experience, then the dance is too hard for them. You can teach anyone anything with enough time, but is it worth the investment. I would rather teach four dances of an appropriate level than one dance that is too hard for them.

There is a long term issue created by teaching the wrong level dance. Invariably it is the harder dances that the dancers will re-request over and over as they try to perfect them. This then lifts the overall level of the class to the point where new dancers cannot integrate into the class. This will eventually lead to the closure of the class as numbers drop off over time. It is better to get the level right first time, or at least try to.

Remember that just because a dance doesn't have any interruptions and is "only" 32 counts, it doesn't mean it is a beginner dance. There are many other factors that make a dance hard or easy.

If you are gathering material from workshops run by guest instructors, be careful of the levels. Because of their heavy appearance schedule, some "celebrity" instructors do not run regular classes. They may not have taught a raw beginner for a very long time. The people they teach at workshops are mostly "petrol head" dancers. These dancers learn quickly, so a dance may appear to the guest instructor to be easy to do. Dances that seem easy at a workshop can be very difficult, when brought back to a class with "regular" dancers.

Researching the Dance

It is important to get the dance right the first time, as correcting a dance after it has already been taught, is both awkward and disruptive. If the dance sheet is incomplete, as many of them are at this stage, many people look to the videos for clarification.

Unless you know what the choreographer looks like, it is difficult to confirm that the people who produced the video know how to interpret the sheet any better than you do. They may have been taught by the choreographer, but then again they probably haven't.

Often it is better to contact the choreographer, if you can, to get clarification rather than trusting the video.

Checking the Music

Make sure the music you have purchased for the dance is the correct version for the dance. Often there are remixes or re-releases that may phrase differently. This may make the Bridges or Restarts not work properly.

Also check if a slower speed piece of music might be required initially. This would allow the dancers get comfortable with the flow of the moves before hitting them with the real music with all the interruptions that may go with that.

As we generally use commercial popular music for our dancing, it is not specifically prepared for dancing. Sometimes the songs have quiet and loud parts. This often means you need to play with the volume of your music source to keep the dancers happy.

There is computer software out there that will allow you to balance out the levels of mp3 files within the song. You can also try to balance the levels of all of your music, so you don't need to make adjustments from song to song.

Know the speed of the target music, and make sure that the tempo you beat cue (see later on for definition) is close to, or working towards the tempo of the target music.

Practicing the Dance

Never go into a class unprepared. Always practice a dance prior to teaching it. This means practicing the dance to the music to find any issues, and also to practice how to explain the steps.

When teaching a dance for the first time I suggest teaching it to your significant other before you go to class. That allows you to get your verbal instructions down pat and it will really help solidify the dance in your mind. That is especially important when teaching multiple new dances each week.

Be willing to explore multiple ways to explain the trickier parts of the choreography, as not everyone will get it the same way.

Changing the Dance

Some instructors take it on themselves to "correct" dances that they are teaching. It is one thing to make a mistake and to teach a dance wrong. It is quite another to deliberately change a dance because you think it would go better a different way.

Your dancers eventually will travel, either within the town they dance in, or within the country, or even overseas. There is a chance that they will see or attempt the same dance elsewhere and face embarrassment when told that they are doing a dance "wrong". It is not the dancers that are "wrong", it is the instructor that changed the dance. You will be found out very quickly, the internet makes the world a very small place in reality.

If you don't want to do the dance the way it was intended, don't do the dance at all. There are plenty of others to choose from out there.

Dance Difficulty Level

Over the years, there has been a vast array of words used to describe the difficulty of a dance. Everything from: "Low Intermediate", "Upper Beginner", Absolute Beginner", "Improver", "Easy/Advanced" etc. None of these seem to be reliable words to interpret. Everyone has their own understanding of what a "beginner" should be capable of. Each individual dancer learns at different speeds, and progresses at their own pace.

What is needed is a reliable measuring of degree of difficulty of choreography. I propose a measuring scale of one to ten, where one is the easiest possible and ten is the hardest possible. By providing a group of classic dances for each of those numbers, I can provide at least an indicator of level that can be interpreted world-wide. Eventually there will be a formula that will calculate the level automatically, however for the moment this system will be more reliable than anything that is currently in use.

Level 1 – Mamma Maria (Trace), Feelin' Kinda Lonely (Swift), 456 Waltz (Hodge)

Level 2 – Crazy Postman (Holt), 98.6 (McKee), Rocket to the Sun (Glover)

Level 3 – Bartender Stomp (Gregory), Ain't Goin' Nowhere (Wong), Peaches and Cream (Metelnick)

Level 4 – September In The Rain (Tripp), The Bomp (Ray), Imelda's Way (Churm)

Level 5 – Silk & Satin (Khinoo), Smokey Places (Perron), Dance Our Way (Heath)

Level 6 – Hot Love (Gallagher), Dream of You (T&V), Islands In The Stream (Jones)

Level 7 – Infinity (Hughes), Pot of Gold (Hrycan), Shakatak (Sala)

Level 8 – Rolling In the Deep (Gallagher), Come Tomorrow (Perron), Shout (Lobos)

Level 9 – Razor Sharp (Sunter), Syncopated Rhythm (Fowler), The Real World (Ruthie)

Level 10 – Anything Much Harder than the ones above

To use this system, look at the dance you want to compare and think: "is this dance harder or easier than the reference dance?" It should allow us to at least get in the right ball park.

Be aware that your opinion of the level may change once you have actually taught it a couple of times. Some dances seem easier than you expect, some harder, for no easily apparent reason. It will pay to make notes on the dance sheet, for future reference when considering dances for revision.

Cueing the Dance

Cueing a dance means saying words with some form of rhythm to assist the dancers in executing the dance steps with the correct timing. There are two methods of verbally cueing a dance. These are "Pre-emptive" cuing and "Beat" cuing.

If you are cueing the dance while the music is playing, as assistance to the dancers, slowly reduce the amount of cueing by the time you get to the end of the second sequence. They did not come to dance to you; they came to dance to the music. If you don't stop, you will be creating a crutch for them and they will become reliant on you permanently. You will also lose the impact of your voice, as they will eventually filter your voice out and ignore you when it becomes really important.

Beat Cuing

Beat Cuing requires the instructor to say a word for each beat or part beat that has an action, to enable the dancers to get used to the timing of the dance. These beats should be given in a regular speed, without fluctuating fast and slow. Effectively, you become the music.

When learning to beat cue it is often useful to buy a metronome from a music shop. This provides a regular beat that can be adjusted for various speeds and provides the instructor with something to practice with. Beat cuing is important to provide the timing of an action, but does not really help the dancers with step knowledge. By the time they hear a word; they will already have had to commit to an action.

The words used to beat cue should be of as few syllables as possible, and should be indicative of the actions required to be executed. "It is impossible to say "Step Right Foot to Right" in one beat, so use the word "Side" instead. The instructor should preferably select a one syllable word that best represents the complete move. If there is a cluster movement that describes the actions, then numbers can be used in place of some actions: For example: "Vine, 2, 3, 4" instead of "Side, Behind, Side, Front".

Sometimes people just don't understand things when you say them one way. It is important to be able to explain things a number of different ways, or beat cue a number of different ways. You can try for a Vine Cha for example:

- Vine 2, 3 and 4
- Slow, Slow, Quick, Quick, Slow
- Vine 2, Cha Cha Cha
- 1, 2, 3 and 4
- Side, Behind, Side, Close, Side

Each way will get through to different people. Try them all.

Be careful of the hyper dancers. They will make you beat cue faster and faster if you don't pull them back in line. Often raising your voice volume and slowing down slightly will assist in retaking control. You are in charge.

If the tempo of the dance is significantly faster than the tempo you are beat cueing, you may want to lift the tempo on the last couple of sequences. Alternatively, do a few more sequences and increase the tempo during those additional sequences.

Developing good breath control is important to get this right, as you also need to fit in taking short shallow breaths when you get a chance. When you do, just leave out the occasional count. Don't leave out more than three counts in a row, as the dancers will lose track.

Pre-Emptive Cuing

Pre-emptive Cuing is only possible if you use cluster terminology, and if your dances are already used to good beat cuing, and can keep in time without assistance. It is a much more difficult skill to develop, and it is worthwhile getting some training from an experienced practitioner (someone who knows how to do it). It requires the instructor to cue key words that describe actions that are about to be done, rather than ones that are already being executed. The timing of saying these cues is critical. If you say it too late, then it is not worth doing and may lead to confusion. If you say it too early, then the dances may start doing the new action before the previous one has been completed, thinking that they are wrong.

If you don't use cluster terminology, then this skill is still useful when warning the dances about interruptions such as Bridges or Restarts.

If you are cueing over the music, it is important to realise when to stop talking and allow them to enjoy the music. Let's face it, that's why they are there, to dance to the music, not your voice. Fade out the voice, and then bring it back in if you see people struggling or getting out of synch with the other dancers.

You will make best use of your impact that way. If you are talking all the time, people will filter you out. Then you won't get any messages across, even when they are important, such as interruptions.

Combined Cuing

Once you have mastered both beat cueing and pre-emptive cueing, it is possible to blend the two. This also assumes that you have good breath control, and the dancers are well trained. This is a difficult skill to master and takes a lot of practice. You also need to leave time to actually breathe as well.

You can interleave the beat cues with pre-emptive cues, or sometimes replace filler words (such as counts) with pre-emptive cues. I definitely recommend seeking mentoring by a skilled professional that has the expertise.

Counting In the Dance

When about to start dancing, it is important that everyone starts at the same time. It is also important that they also all start at the same speed. In an orchestra, this job is done by the conductor, in a band it is usually the drummer's job. To do this in line dancing the instructor or DJ uses a technique called "Counting In". This is also important when walking a dance through without the music, so everyone starts together.

There should be at least three words used to count in. My personal preference is "Ready, 2, 3, Go" (others use 5,6,7,8) for common time and "Ready, 2, Go" (others use 4,5,6) for Waltz Time. The dancing starts on the next beat after the "Go". The time spacing between the words gives the dancers an indication of how fast you want them to "Go". If you say them quickly, the dancers will expect to continue the actions quickly. You should then follow the count in with Beat Cuing that is of the same tempo.

The only time I do not count in is when I am walking through a piece of choreography for the very first time. This is the only time that the timing of the moves is not important.

Counting in is essential when everyone is facing away from you and therefore cannot see you are about to move. It is easier to get them in the habit of waiting for it all of the time, and then it won't matter where you are in the room, even sitting down with a broken leg (heaven forbid).

Counting in is also essential when starting with the music. The dancers may have never heard the song before, so have no idea when the lyrics start, nor if that is the right spot to start anyway.

Before counting in, it is wise to remind them which foot is to be used to start. If they have been standing still for any length of time, their weight will be on both feet and invariably someone will go the wrong way.

Reading a Dance Sheet while Teaching

This is a pet peeve of many people. It may not look very professional to be holding a dance sheet while teaching a class. However, it is also very unprofessional to frequently get something wrong, and have to go over and check a detail before continuing. This all comes from lack of preparation. Know your material before teaching it, or don't teach it at all.

It is a different matter when it comes to doing requests in class, or at a social, or when revising an old dance you haven't danced for a long time. It is impossible to store the thousands of dances you have done, in your memory, and recall them accurately every time. Having a sheet available as a refresher is critical in this situation.

It is this sort of situation that having a quick cue version of each dance sheet is very valuable. It saves having to wade through all of the small details of a dance each time, providing it is accurate and concise.

Theoretical Competency and Training Models

There are many theoretical studies into how people learn new skills. I have included three of them here for interest sake. Use what you think works, to understand and recognise your customer's needs and abilities. I have modified the descriptions into the context of line dancing from the original geek speak.

Four Stages of Competency

When people learn any skill, they develop through four different stages of competency. These levels are:

- Unconscious Incompetence – The dancer does not understand or know how to line dance, but doesn't necessarily realise that they don't know. "It's easy; I'll just do it with everyone else". Hopefully they will move out of this stage very quickly, but some don't.
- Conscious Incompetence – The dancer does not know how to line dance, but realises that they don't know and are willing to learn. They realise that making mistakes is part of the learning process.
- Conscious Competence – The dancer knows how to line dance, but demonstrating the dancing requires high levels of concentration.
- Unconscious Competence – The dancer has had so much practice that line dancing has become second nature and can be performed while doing or thinking about something else. This dancer may be able to teach it to, or assist others depending on how and when it was learned.

It is important to recognise at what stage each individual is at, and help them progress through to the end, or put them in a position on the dance floor to assist them in progressing, or helping others.

Fits & Posner's Three Stages of Motor Learning

Motor learning is training the body to learn a new physical movement skill. The body and brain go through three stages as it absorbs and refines the knowledge.

- Cognitive Stage – This stage is when the new dancer sees others doing the action and tries to understand what is required to do it themselves. Their actions will be clumsy and awkward.
- Associative Stage – This stage is when the new dancer develops a more refined, less clumsy form of action, and is starting to absorb "how" to do something, rather than just "what" to do.
- Autonomous Stage – This final stage of learning is when the action becomes mostly automatic even in an unpredictable environment like a social or workshop.

There is no point telling a person in the cognitive stage of learning an action about the fine execution details, until they have achieved the fundamental action. There is no point pushing a dancer to go to a social or crowded environment until well into the associative stage, it will only scare them.

Dreyfus Model of Increased Skill Development

The Drefus Model describes five roles of skill learning:

1. Novice – Rigidly adheres to taught movements and doesn't think of changing anything.
2. Advanced Beginner – Each movement is treated as a separate item, with limited changing of body mechanics to suit the relationship to other actions before or after.
3. Competent – Copes with multiple movements impacting each other and understands flow. Plans ahead and can absorb large chunks.
4. Proficient – Understands variations from normal clusters and how they will affect the general flow of the actions. Can adapt known clusters to handle new situations. Can picture an overall view of the choreography.
5. Expert/Master – Has a vision of what is possible and can analyse new situations and can create new rules and terminology to cover those situations. They can intuitively handle any complex choreographic concept and make sense of it.

Most dancers get to the "Competent" role. They need to be "Proficient" before attempting to become an instructor. This model may help you in determining if a dancer has stopped becoming a beginner, and is ready to move on to harder challenges.

It is important for an instructor to realise that, even though they may have an aspiration to be the most proficient dancer they can be, not everyone else has the same desire. Many dancers are happy to be average and just have fun. There is nothing wrong with that, it is a personal choice, and is affected by everything else in their busy lives.

Voice Production

Even though you are probably using some form of amplification, projecting your voice effectively is still very important. Amplification can only reproduce what goes in one end and make it louder. Apart from tone adjustment, it cannot fix problems that exist in the original voice.

The following information is based on an article by Graham Williamson, a retired Speech Pathologist in the UK. For a more detailed description, go to his website www.sltinfo.com. It is very informative on the subject.

Effective voice production is the combination of three factors:
- Appropriate breathing techniques
- Easy onset of the vibration of the vocal chords
- Projection of the voice without strain or pushing

Breathing Techniques

The most recommended breathing technique is Diaphragmatic breathing, also known as abdominal breathing or tummy breathing:

There are three steps to abdominal breathing:
- Yawn
- Breath IN as your tummy moves out
- Breath OUT as your tummy moves in

The yawn should be gentle, as a gentle yawn is relaxing for the throat. It serves to open the back of the throat to allow the passage of air in and out. As you get better at the technique, you can extend the time of breathing out, over the time of breathing in. Importantly though, you should not strain the muscles, do it gently.

Easy Onset

When we vocalise sounds, our vocal folds vibrate. Ideally they should vibrate in an easy, relaxed manner without forcing or straining them. Often the chords are brought together too harshly at the beginning of some words, especially when the word begins with a vowel sound. This is called Hard Attack.

Hard Attack, rather like clearing your throat, can potentially traumatise the vocal chords causing inflammation, swelling and localised irritation. Effective voice production requires the elimination of Hard Attack, and the substitution of the opposite – Easy Onset.

Easy Onset is achieved by ensuring the vocal tract is relaxed and open, without excessive muscle tension around the neck area. There is a simple way to practice this technique by placing the sound 'h' in front of words that begin with vowel sounds.

For example: Try saying "Annie ate an apple" aloud. If you find you are hitting the vowels at the beginning of the words with too much force, try putting a 'h' in front of each word. Ie. h-Annie h-ate h-an h-apple. Say the 'h' for a prolonged time, then, with practice, reduce the length, till you are not forcing the vocal folds together.

Voice Projection

Using these previous breathing and easy onset techniques, coupled with the following will assist in much better voice projection:

- Relaxation of the head, neck and shoulder muscles
- Good posture, keep your head up and shoulders back
- No straining, your voice is strongest when you relax

Your good posture allows your upper chest as a resonator to amplify the sound without straining.

It is wise to be taught safely to project your voice by a qualified person, but these exercises should help provide a foundation for good projection, with adequate volume.

Teaching Techniques
Dancer Learning Styles

Each person has their own preferences on how they learn best. This will often determine where they prefer to stand in a class, and by moving them, you actually will affect how effectively they will learn.

There are seven main learning styles are:
- Visual – The dancer prefers to see what is required
- Aural – The dancer prefers to just put on the music and try it
- Verbal – The dancer prefers to hear an explanation
- Kinaesthetic (Physical) – The dancer prefers to just do it
- Logical – The dancer wants to understand why and how
- Social – The dancer prefers to learn with a group of dancers
- Solitary – The dancer prefers to work it out alone

Everyone is able to learn from all these methods, but will have a dominant preference. Some styles will work in a small group, but will not work for a large crowd. Each style has its own advantages and disadvantages. As an instructor it is important to be able to take advantage of all the teaching methods available to you to get the message across as efficiently as possible.

The main three styles used in line dance teaching are: Verbal, Visual and Physical. We explain, we show and we do. Approximately 40% of people are dominant visual learners, 50% are dominant physical learners and only 10% are dominant verbal learners.

Verbal learners need to be told what to do, they need clear, precise, consistent instructions; for example specify which foot a step should be done with (such as right heel, close) because the verbal learner will probably not be standing in a position where they can see your feet. A dominant verbal learner will not learn easily just by watching.

The verbal method of teaching has been sadly underdeveloped in line dancing due to the lack of standard terminology up to this point. When teachers use ambiguous or overloaded words to describe things, it makes it hard for the dancer to understand clearly what is required without visual clarification.

Visual learners however, learn almost totally by watching you. They will usually be your front row dancers. If a dancer who stands near the back of the room is constantly asking you to show them something again because they couldn't see, they are probably a visual learner and you should suggest they try standing closer to the front of the room. Visual learners need sharp, well defined steps to follow.

At this point I should mention exaggeration of footwork. As an instructor you should exaggerate your footwork to make it easier for dancers to follow, however, you should explain to the dancers that you are exaggerating and they should not try to take large steps like you.

If you have a stage at your venue, then showing works well, as you are elevated and everyone can see. If not, then those past the first couple of rows can't see, and therefore won't learn from the demonstration. Anything that gets to the back people will be filtered using the "Chinese whisper" effect, as they see someone interpret what they saw, rather than the original demonstration.

Kinaesthetic learners learn by doing. Whilst they may pick up a certain amount by watching and listening, they will really only totally learn a sequence by doing it. Kinaesthetic learners are easy to spot. When you say "Just watch me, don't do this", they are the ones who will do it anyway! They learn by repetition and will be the dancers most likely to ask for another walk through before you put the music on.

Most people use a combination of all three learning styles. It is very rare to come across someone who uses only one style of learning. This simply means that it may take several weeks of observation before you can identify the dominant learning style of each dancer. As with all the other skills you acquire as an instructor, you will get better at it with practice.

By knowing about the different learning styles you can check your teaching methods. Ask yourself, "Am I catering to all learning styles? Can I improve any part of my technique to better cater for a particular style?"

Moving Around the Class

If you are not working from a stage, then you have the opportunity to teach from various parts of the dance floor. This can be useful when it is a particularly complex group of moves that do not have a cluster name.

They say a picture is worth a thousand words. Sometime demonstrating, while explaining, will get the message across much quicker than explaining alone. This ideally should be done where the dancers are facing. You have the option to temporarily turn them to face the stage if necessary, but nothing beats facing the way it is going to be done the first time.

If there is a large crowd and no stage, you may need to repeat the demonstration at various parts of the dance floor, rather than just down the back. Some people rotate the rows back, so everyone gets a chance to see, but this can be very disruptive and time consuming.

It can also be useful if there are not many experienced dancers around. Usually the experienced dancers migrate to the front. This leaves the back and corner regions sometimes full of weaker dancers. I find it beneficial to teach from a weaker corner or from the back sometimes, to improve the strength of the weaker areas.

This actually improves the front row as well, as they are often addicted to seeing the instructor, and should learn to be less reliant on their visual skills.

Muscle Memory

Many people think that the only memory they have is in their head. Though this brain memory is very important, there is also what is called muscle memory. When a person repeats an activity over and over it becomes instinctive. All the muscles get used to the activity and the brain is no longer needed to concentrate on coordinating the actions.

As a dance teacher you can take advantage of this memory. Repeat a specific task over and over at least four times, preferably more. If it is not a move that can be repeated because it comes out on the wrong foot, then make up a little routine that enables the move to be repeated with as little other stuff around it as possible.

If the dancer can accomplish that task, and be able to ask the person alongside their middle name (for example), then they have trained their auto-pilot and can move on.

Chunking

When teaching a dance it is usually necessary to break the complete choreography into manageable pieces or "chunks". Each piece is taught over and over, till the dancers are competent. The "chunks" are assembled to form larger chunks, till the whole dance sequence has been taught. Only then do you attempt to do the dance to other walls.

Choosing the Chunks

Occasionally you may want to use the music for just a chunk of the dance to get a "feel" for the dance, but this is an inefficient use of time as there is nearly always lead-in music before the dance starts.

The size of the individual chunks is chosen by the instructor based on the complexity of the dance, and the capability of the dancers. Usually the chunks are 8 or 16 beats in length for Common Time dances and 6 or 12 beats in length for Waltz Time dances. If there is a lot of symmetry, then the chunks may be longer.

If you include symmetry in a chunk, you will reduce the teach time. By doing something and then immediately doing it again on the other foot, you will likely get a "Freebie". A Freebie" is a piece of choreography that does not need to be taught, as they can already do it. If you use consistent cluster terminology from dance to dance, you will benefit from many Freebies along the way. Then all you need to teach are the uncommon bits, any unusual timing in the dance, and the overall sequence of clusters.

Be aware however, that sometimes doing something on the left foot won't work as well as doing it on the right foot. Kick Ball Changes and Monterey Turns are typical examples of this, as they are rarely done on the left foot.

Sometimes the place to break the chunk is not simple, and may be based on cluster terms or symmetry of the choreography. Break the chunk wherever you consider is easiest to explain to the dancers. This may not be where the chunk is specified on the dance sheet in the head cues.

Assembling the Chunks

When reassembling the chunks, it is important not to overdo the early chunks and underdo the later chunks. If a dance is broken into four chunks (call them A, B, C and D), then the process of assembly for the dance should be as follows:

- Teach Key Clusters (see later on)
- Teach A
- Teach B
- Walk A + B
- Teach C
- Walk B + C
- (Optional) Walk A + B + C
- Teach D
- Walk C + D + start of A
- 1st Wall – Walk A + B + C + D + start of A
- 2nd Wall – Walk A + B + C + D + start of A
- 1st Wall – Walk A + B + C + D + A + ... for Minimum of 4 full Sequences
- (Optional) Do it all to non-phrased slow music (not proper track)
- Teach Interruptions
- Walk Each "Dance Bit + Interruption + Dance Bit" scenario at the correct wall
- Do it to music (maybe slowed down)
- Do it to music correct speed (possibly twice)

A very important part of this assembly process is practicing the "glue". The "glue" is the join between the chunks. When a chunk is being practiced, allow the chunk to flow a beat or two into the next chunk (if they know it already) to enable the body mechanics to be experienced and practiced.

This will reduce the surprises when the whole dance is assembled. Most latent issues will be found at the joins, usually between the end of the sequence and the start of the following sequence.

When you get to the point that you are gluing together complete sequences, tell them to "keep going". Otherwise they will be in the habit of stopping, and will assume you will be stopping again.

When it comes to dancing to the music, dance it at least twice in a row. The first time it is likely to be clumsy and erratic with many mistakes. By the second time it will be smoother, and they will actually feel like they are dancing. You may even want to do it a third time, but be aware of the length of the song. If it is over three and a half minutes, you are probably pushing it a bit far. If it is a short dance to a long song, then probably once is enough.

Walking Through, compared to Teaching

There is a difference between teaching a dance and "walking through" a dance. A walk through assumes that the dancers have already done the dance previously and just need a reminder. The chunks may be larger, and the number of repeated sequences attempted, before the music is used, is likely to be fewer.

Providing Directional Reference Points

It is important to explain what names you will use to describe the walls of your venue. Front and back are fairly obvious, but are words already used as part of the step terminology so are overloaded. Possibly use "Stage" and "Road" or some such instead. For the other walls use words that relate to some visible object, such as a piano, or an exit. Often it is useful to name corners as well, when doing dances that use the diagonals or do 1/8 turns.

Do not say "face this wall" and point your finger. People at the back may not be able to see you. Give the directions relevant names.

Spotting

Many people get dizzy when trying to do some of the turns the choreographers put into their dances. Dizziness occurs when we observe things moving past us during a turn. A technique that can be used to reduce this comes from Ballet originally and is called spotting. You concentrate your eyes on one point on the wall, then, while executing the turn leave the eyes pointing at that spot until no longer possible. At that point quickly whip the head around until you can see that spot again. I do not recommend that you do it too vigorously to start with, as you might put your neck out with whiplash, but it does work. Just go fast enough to blur the objects that pass you, and don't try to focus on them. Slowly build up your neck muscles.

As a lower impact version of this, you can also reduce the impact of multiple consecutive alternating turns. Work out the target wall after all the turns will be completed, find a spot on that wall, then watch it, allowing the body to turn but reduce the head turning. This will reduce the amount of dizziness generated.

Partial spotting requires spotting two objects, one the opposite direction to the other. This can be used for slower more gradual turns as you switch from one spot to the other.

Creating Choreography Options

Some dancers suffer from conditions that make turning or twisting difficult. This can be caused through vertigo or other illnesses of the ear. It can also be due to hip, knee or ankle injuries or illnesses.

Often the instructor has the ability to recommend "low impact" or "low turn" alternative steps to replace the jumping, twisting or turning parts of the dance. This enables the instructor to fulfil a "duty of care" to the customers. It is important that the replacement chunk has the same traffic pattern and travel as the chunk it is replacing. Otherwise the non-turners will be in the wrong position with respect to the people executing the dance correctly. The non-turn option should also flow into the next piece of choreography as well as possible.

Reading Body Language (Kinesics)

Many of the dancers are frightened or insecure about asking for something to be explained again. Others are unwilling to admit to making a mistake or not understanding something. You seem to need to be a mind reader in this business.

There are some things that you can watch for that give you signs that you need to address something. This is often called non-verbal communication or technically Kinesics (kin-ee-sicks). Many body language experts and sources seem to agree that between 50-80% of all human communications are non-verbal. Some useful examples are:

- Lack of eye contact and other eye movement
- Slouching of the shoulders or lowering of the head
- Facial expression indicating guilt or surprise
- Minimising of actions. Unsure people will take smaller steps
- Relationship to other people. If two dancers are dancing closer together than the others, one may have made a mistake to get to that position.

In the line dance environment, some of these are harder to catch, as most of the time, there is no face to face contact with the dances while they are dancing. You learn to read the backs of their heads and posture instead.

Picking on Dancers

Some instructors like to single individual dancers out for comments, criticism or assistance. This can lighten up a class, and it can destroy it, with only a few words. Be very, very careful.

If you are going to single someone out, you need to be aware that they can handle it. Not everyone is comfortable with individual attention in a group environment. You also need to be able to take it back when they reply, either in anger or jest.

Unless you know the each individual in the class well, I recommend you refrain from this sort of thing, and just practice on, and with, the class clown.

Things Not to Do

Here is a list of things that you should not do, if you want to keep the dancers happy.

- Never show or tell the dancers a piece of choreography that you **do not** want them to do. All it does is put the idea in their head and they will have difficulties removing it. Just reinforce what you **do** want them to do. Stop other dancers from doing this as well (treat it as a joke, rather than a telling off).
- Do not teach more than one dance to any particular piece of music, unless the original dance has been deleted from the class play list at least ten years. If teaching another dance for a split floor, keep the levels of the two dances at least three difficulty levels apart. All you do otherwise is confuse the dancer's subconscious. If it is a different artist doing the same song, then that may be alright, but be cautious.
- Never use the word "and" when beat cueing a dance, unless it means an "&" count (half beat) in the music.
- Do not avoid teaching a dance just because you do not like the choreographer. It is the dancers that miss out, and your professional reputation that is damaged, not the choreographers.
- Do not pretend you have not made a mistake if you did. The dancers communicate with each other and it's better to confess and make a joke of it. We are all human, well most of us anyway. If you taught a dance wrong, correct it as soon as you are aware, assuming that you do the dance again.
- Do not let a dancer intimidate you into teaching a dance that you know is outside their level, or the level of the rest of the class. Once you teach something, you can't take it away, without looking foolish. Stand your ground, explain your principals and wear the onslaught.
- If you see a dancer showing another dancer a move, do not presume they are being disruptive. They may have been asked how a move goes and are just responding. You may deal with it if it becomes a regular thing with the same dancer, but do it in private.
- Never get angry at the dancers to their faces. Save it till they are gone.
- Never tell the class gossip anything you do not want the world to know. Remember it probably goes both ways.
- Do not ask two questions at once, it only confuses them. "Did you like that, or was it too fast?" should be broken into two separate questions if you want a useful answer from a group of dancers.

- If you see someone struggling through a bit in a walk through, do not assume "they will get it eventually". You are the teacher, work out what is wrong and fix it.
- Do not bring your personal life to the dance floor, unless it is humorous. These are not family, nor friends. They are paying customers. They come to dance class to get away from their personal issues, and don't need to take on yours. Especially keep it from the microphone.
- Don't tell the dancers that something is hard. You then set up a mental block that will make it so, whether it really was or not.

Describing an Action

When teaching steps, it is important to use your words efficiently. The more you say, the less people will listen. They just seem to tune out. Some people seem to be able to talk without actually getting any message across. I call it "verbal diarrhoea".

Standardising the order you say things will assist in getting the message across. The sentence "Step the Right Foot Forward" is more helpful than "Right Foot Forward and Step. Tell them "what to do", tell them "what to do it with", and tell them "where to do it".

Reduce the amount of "fluff" words in the teaching. "We are going to step the right foot forward, then we are going to bring the left foot up to the right foot and then step the right foot alongside the left foot and change weight to the left foot" is really bad but rather common unfortunately. "Step right foot forward, close left foot with weight" achieves the same thing in way less time and effort.

When is it Too Much Detail?

If you give people too much information that they don't need, you can be thought of as condescending, rather than being helpful. It can be a fine line trying to decide how much to push a point and when to back off. It is a very subtle issue and hard to measure. It really is just a matter of experience and knowing your customers.

Keep an eye on the second to weakest dancer to know when to stop teaching and move on. You need to be flexible enough to change your teaching descriptions if the customers change. If new people are added, then increase the amount of detailed descriptions. If there are no new people then decrease the amount of detailed descriptions.

Cueing a Move

Each action requires its own specific explanation to get the message across. The more you teach them, the more efficient you will become at explaining common actions. The sooner you teach them the terminology that goes with an action, the sooner you can use it to save time. For example: "Step the right foot alongside the left foot changing weight to the right foot... this is called a Close". From then on you can refer to it as a close.

Each move is executed on a beat or a part beat. For you to put moves together to create clusters you will need to pick a word, preferably a single syllable word, that best describes the move. Then you are able to string the moves together, on their respective beats or part beats, to provide the timing of the cluster.

As there are likely to be multiple actions and turns in each move, you will need to prioritise the information to get the most beneficial outcome from the dancers. You have already described in detail each move, so all you are now doing is providing a reference word to trigger the actions for the dancers. You should have thought of this while teaching the actions, so you can embed the key word into the teaching description.

Describing a Turn in a Cluster

With turns I have found that it is sometimes easier to let the dancer work it out than go into too much depth. This goes against my normal philosophy, but in this case it usually works. Get them to try, and then correct any issues. Sort of using the KISS principal... "Keep It Simple Stupid". Tell them to travel left, turn full left and take 3 steps.... Go. If that doesn't work you can break it down into ¼, ½, ¼, but you may find you don't need to (if you are lucky).

Basic body mechanics is likely to make them do the turn the way that feels most comfortable to them, which should be the way the choreographer intended as well.

Describing a Cluster

When teaching clusters, it is important to reinforce the cluster family relationship. If there are modified clusters, teach the parent cluster first (on the correct foot), then explain what modifications are needed to do the cluster being used in this particular dance.

Add each modification one at a time in whatever order makes sense to you, until the fully modified cluster is achieved. Once they are familiar with the modified cluster, then you may be able to stop mentioning the modifications when pre-emptive cuing, without them going wrong.

Using clusters is a very efficient way of getting additional body mechanic or styling information across to the dancers. Once they are familiar with the parent cluster, then you get a lot of freebies down the track.

If the dance uses a parent cluster without any modifiers, do not add unnecessary modifiers. It just confuses the dancers and pollutes your teaching message. For example:

- There is no "Back Coaster", a coaster is always back unless specified otherwise.
- There is no "Closed Twinkle", a twinkle is always closed unless specified otherwise.
- There is no "Closed Scissor", a scissor is always closed unless specified otherwise.
- There is no "Side Chasse", a chasse is always sideways unless specified otherwise.
- There is no "Forward Kick", a kick is always forward unless specified otherwise.
- There is no "Side Point", a point is always to the side unless specified otherwise.

If there is additional styling, or upper body work with a cluster, it is advisable to add them after the fundamental actions are mastered. Sometimes however, claps and clicks make a cluster easier to do. The human brain is an amazing thing, go with whatever works for you.

You will eventually create a personal method of describing each cluster that works for you. Here is mine for a "1/4 Turning Jazz 3, Close".

"Imagine you are stepping into four corners of a square or box on the floor below you. Now starting with the right foot, step onto the top left corner of the box. Step the left foot back into the bottom left corner of the box. Step the right foot sideways onto the bottom right corner of the box. Now step the left foot forward onto the top right hand corner of the box. Now you try it… Cross, Back, Side, Forward, Cross Back, Side, Forward. That is a Jazz Box. Now in this dance, we don't do the last step forward. Instead we Close alongside We call it a Jazz 3, Close. So .. try it .. Cross, Back, Side, Close, Cross, Back, Side, Close, Jazz, 2, 3, Close. Notice you are drifting diagonally back. Don't worry, that's normal. Now we are going to change it further. While doing the Jazz 3 we are going to incorporate a ¼ turn. You try it …"

You may need to practice saying some of the terminology before using them in front of dancers. "Slow Sailor Shuffle" is one such term that takes practice. It is a bit of a tongue twister. There are a number of verbal slips that are common and quite funny (or embarrassing in some company). "Toe Struts" can become "Toe Sluts" for example.

When you first teach a cluster, you will mention each of the primary actions, but as they get familiar with it, it is important to brainwash them with the cluster name. Incorporate the "Jazz, 2, 3, 4" after a couple of "Cross, Back, Side, Forward", so they can grasp the connection between the cluster name and its related actions.

If a cluster can be repeated over and over, it is often a good idea to do that, even if it is not repeated immediately in the dance. This teaches the muscle memory. Once they have it, then you can cut it back to what is actually in the dance. Just make sure that the cluster you want to repeat actually comes out on the foot you need to do it over and over. If it doesn't, then consider whether using the opposite foot version is giving them too much information at the time, or whether it will be of benefit later in the dance.

This works well with paddles, montana kicks, vaudevilles etc. Tell them that you want more than one before launching into it though, as they will stop otherwise. Look at them to see that they have the cluster before moving on. If need be, turn them to face the back so you can see if they have got it.

Once you have defined a move or a cluster, make sure you continue to use the terminology after that point, so they get used to it.

Describing a Chunk

When putting a chunk together, make sure you cover all the beats of the chunk, including the Holds. They need to feel the pattern from start to end, which includes all the timing,

If you want to take advantage of symmetry, then don't stop them in between. Try saying: "now do the same on the other foot" and keep them flowing. Their auto-pilots might save you teaching time. Don't say "repeat that", if it is on the other foot, as they may try to do it with the same foot. Save the word repeat for identical repeats.

When walking through a chunk, remind the dancers where you want to start, before taking off. You might know where you want to start, but unless you tell them, they won't know until too late.

By the time you get to this point, you shouldn't need to teach or cue the individual actions. All of the clusters that make up the chunk have been explained, including the timing. Once you mention which foot you are starting the chunk, you should be able to use the momentum from move to move to guarantee the correct foot will be used. This is the most efficient way to get the message across. You should just cue the individual move key words to ensure the timing is followed.

Teaching a Dance

Sometimes it pays to workshop a few of the key clusters of a dance or even of a chunk, before starting to teach the chunks at all. This enables you to teach the muscle memory for that particular key piece of the dance. If you wait till it occurs in the walk through, then all you have taught before the key move will be forgotten by the time you have handled the key move.

You can reuse the knowledge of clusters from previous dances in the session, but if there are new dancers to the class, you cannot assume knowledge from previous sessions.

Remember, a house will not stay up without a good foundation. If you don't teach the fundamentals properly, then the overall teach of the dance will fail.

Often with the simpler dances, you can teach the whole dance without a turn first. This enables the dancers to see you while they struggle with the choreographic concepts. Once they are comfortable with the dance, then you can add the turn.

If you are adding a turn, explain where the intended end of the turn is expected to face. It is here that having the wall (and sometimes corner) names is important for quick reference.

Make sure you add the start to the end as soon as you have finished the last chunk of the dance. Just a couple of beats will do, but that "glue" is an important part of the dance.

Keep it slow and steady till they have the structure and then you can speed it up slowly, till they are ready for the tempo of the music, or the slow speed that you intend to use first.

At the conclusion of teaching a dance, it helps to get a quick survey of whether they liked the dance or not. Once you get a feel for what that particular class like, it will assist in selecting new dances, and help in picking requests or revision dances.

It really is all about minimising the time taken and words used and maximising the information given to make your explanation as efficient as possible.

Fixing a dancer's mistake

When a dancer makes a mistake during some part of the teach, or walk through. Do not immediately pull them up and correct it. Some people learn by doing, and need to make the mistake to learn how to correct it.

Wait till you see the mistake repeated, before addressing it. If you do address it, try doing it as a general correction, rather than singling out the individual. If they don't get the hint after another opportunity, you can either chose to:

- Ignore it and move on
- Fix it immediately with the chance of embarrassing the dancer
- Fix it privately afterwards (especially if it is not too serious)

It helps to know the individuals, and if they are happy for direct critique in front of others. Often it pays to ask people you don't know well before critiquing them.

All Eyes are on You!

Be aware that your dancers are watching your every move. If you are walking through a small chunk over and over, you may want to see if they have got it. To do this you have to turn your head or your whole body to see. Warn them you are going to turn around and you want them to keep going. Otherwise they will turn around with you, creating chaos.

Alternatively, have them face the back wall, and get them to repeat the sequence facing that way, so you can see any issues.

I have made the mistake in a large class of over a hundred people, whereby I was unsure of the next step, so I leant over to look at my sheet, turned around, and there were over a hundred people leaning over with me.

When do I move on?

When teaching a dance to a group of dancers, everyone will catch on at different speeds. You will always have someone who gets it first, and someone who gets it last (or doesn't get it at all).

Monitor the amount of repeats you do of clusters, chunks and sequences. If you wait till the last person has got the piece that you are teaching, you may be frustrating the ones that got it first. At some point you must decide when to move on, even if some of the dancers have not yet grasped the concept you are describing.

You need to consider if you have given the weaker dancer a fair chance at it. Remember that some people learn by doing, so may eventually get it when you are repeating the concept later on. Some people attempt to dance outside their experience level, without consideration for the others in the class, or consideration for the instructor.

I recommend you watch the weakest two dancers, and move on when the second to weakest dancer has grasped the concept. Do not be intimidated by the stronger dancers, but be considerate of them.

Not everyone wants to achieve!

I know I have mentioned this before, but it is probably the most important message in this book to instructors and potential instructors. Even though you might want to do the higher level dances and achieve the pinnacle of line dancing, many people do not.

The general dancer is often motivated by exercise, social contact or music enjoyment, far more than the challenge of the dancing. You cannot force customers to do what they do not want to do. They will just leave.

Not everyone wants to excel, not all dancers want to do the hardest dances. Many people have lots of stress in their personal and professional careers. They don't need or want it in their social dancing as well. I estimate that this may be as many as eighty percent of potential dancers you will lose, if you push them too high.

They might want to get there eventually, but their speed of progress should be at their choice, rather than an arbitrary decision made by an impatient instructor.

How can I teach someone rhythmically challenged?

This is probably the hardest issue you will have to deal with as a beginner level instructor. It is harder in line dancing than other forms of dancing, because there is no partner to assist in keeping the student in time.

It is likely to require some special private tuition and perseverance. Fortunately it doesn't happen very often. Obviously this can't be done in class, as it will distract the other dancers. Remember, start slowly and then speed up when they have got it.

Ideally you will need a metronome (you can get one from a music shop), and around five pieces of music that the student is familiar with and enjoys listening to. Try to ensure that the music has a slow enough beat (around 80 to 100 bpm to start with), and that the beat is distinct, without too many secondary beats to distract the student. Make sure that the rhythm is actually standard rhythm and not waltz rhythm. When each stage of the system works, try it to the other pieces of music before moving on.

There are two parts to this learning exercise. First you need to teach the pulse of the music. This is the individual beats irrespective of phrasing in the music. Secondly you need to teach the rhythm, which is being able to recognise the primary or down beat for each measure of music.

To get the pulse, try a clapping or tapping (with a pencil on a table) exercise. Clap with them along with the metronome, or music, so they can hear the example, and then you stop clapping, and see if their solo clapping still stays in pulse with the music or metronome. This helps them feel the beat.

Once that works, then you can get them to count out loud the beats 1,2,3,4, again at the same time as you. This will help them find the down beat or primary beat of each measure which will usually match with step clusters when dancing. If they are nervous about counting out loud, return to the clap/tap exercise, but make the 1 count more prominent or louder.

Once they have the primary count happening, then they can try walking to the same music. Nothing complex, just walking.

When that happens consistently then…. Dancing…

Keep it simple first. Just do a Box cluster… over and over. Move on when ready….

Class Structure

I find that dancers can concentrate for not much longer than thirty minutes before needing a break. Do not be intimidated by the hyper and economist dancers, the breaks are important for the social aspect of the line dance class. It is also important that everyone stays hydrated, so they need a drink break anyway. It shouldn't be any more than ten minutes, and is usually no more than five, about every thirty minutes.

Levels of Classes

Where possible, I recommend that a line dance class is given a specific level and only choreography appropriate for that level is introduced to that class. I suggest the levels should be called: Easy, Mainstream, Challenge and Advanced.

- Easy – Many instructors would call this "Beginner" or worse "Absolute Beginner". I do not think that this is fair to the many people that attend these level classes and have decided that they do not want the stress of anything harder. It is an entry level that should be maintained as a continuous intake class, rather than as a short term training class. I recommend dance levels 1, 2 and 3 for this level of class.
- Mainstream – This level is the standard level that most people attain. Often called "Improver" I do not think that is a nice name to call a level, and implies that they are "not quite there yet". It should be achievable within a couple of years and provides interesting

routines without high levels of turns or complexities. I recommend dance levels 4 and 5 for this level of class.

- Challenge – Even though the word Intermediate is embedded in line dancing, I don't think it's a great descriptor. The word intermediate still implies you are between somewhere and somewhere else. Dances at this Challenge level are more complex with more turns, longer sequences and more complex timing. I recommend dance levels 6 and 7 for this level of class.

- Advanced – Dances for the line dance addicts, and the physically and mentally flexible dancers. These dances are not for everyone, but provide even more challenge for those who want to be stretched. I recommend dance levels 8 and above for this level of class.

I realise the idea of capping the level of a class could be considered controversial and also may be impossible in remote areas. It means there are fabulous pieces of choreography out there that you will not get to teach or learn. However that will always be the case. You cannot do everything out there that exists. It is best to choose dances that are appropriate for the people in the class, and be comfortable with that decision. You don't need to tell anyone you are holding material back.

Setting a Teaching Programme

Apart from the first couple of weeks of a new class (when everything is new), it is unwise to plan more than one new dance a week. Each new dance should be danced for at least two weeks before dropping it from the thorough teach list.

I also find that having a revision week every five weeks is also worthwhile. Cover the dances that were introduced over the previous four weeks.

For an Easy level class, I recommend starting with a level 1 dance, followed by a level 2 dance followed by two level 3 dances. If it is a fairly new class, then you may want to drop the level 3 dances and add in more level 2 dances. I also recommend for these classes that there is only one new dance every two weeks.

For experienced classes, I recommend planning four dances for thorough teaching in a 2 hour class, with any left over time spent on requests. The first dance should be an easier warmup dance, and the last dance in the programme an old classic dance to be reviewed. The other two dances would be the new dance, and the previous week's new dance. Any left over time can be used to do requests from the dancers on the floor.

Remember, if a dance takes more than 30 minutes to teach, then it is not appropriate for that class.

Being flexible is also very important however. You can plan as much as you like, but once the dancers walk through the door, you may need to quickly review the plan and adjust it to compensate for any unexpected situations.

When doing requests, it is likely some dancers will come up with weird and unusual choices sometimes, which you are unprepared for. If you need preparation time, then ask for requests for the following weeks programme, and keep a running request list from week to week.

Others will always ask for the same request over and over and over. If you find some individuals or specific dances dominate the requests to the exclusion of others, then use a list of names of attendees to select the requester in alphabetic order. This will ensure the silent majority get an opportunity. They can always say "pass" if they don't want one (but most will).

If they all keep requesting the harder end of the spectrum then impose an alternating request system between easier and harder dances. If they persist in insisting on hard dances, inject some easy ones of your own. Remember, it is your class.

If you start a class season with a large number of dancers, and loose most of them before the end of the season, then something is very wrong. Usually you are teaching beyond their level, or your teaching skills need improving. Get some advice from a successful mentor.

It is important to plan your individual session structure before starting the class. Keep the selection of dances as varied as possible. Vary the rhythms, vary the tempos, vary the difficulties and vary the styles of the dances to avoid boredom or saturation of the brain.

Be ready to adapt if you notice issues developing, and use the same thoughts when it comes to selecting from the requests from the dancers. Don't put too many of the same style of dance together. For example: don't put two waltzes together.

Music and Line Dance

Emotional Connections

In many people music is more than just entertaining noise. Many people have an emotional connection with specific songs or tunes that featured during their many life experiences. It may remind them of an event, a person or just a feeling. Sometimes these connections can be quite powerful. I have had people run out of my class crying for no apparent reason. I would later find out that the particular song was one that they used to dance to with their late husband, or it was played at a close friend's funeral.

It is difficult to not play a song that the other people enjoy so much, but it pays to be considerate of the people that it might upset. Prepare them if you know of a pending issue. Many sufferers of this condition want to get through it, but it is often an unexpected and powerful wave of emotion the first time.

It is worthwhile to occasionally survey your dancers for their music tastes, providing the class is not too large to make this impractical. Do not assume that if someone is old that they like just old music. They come to class to be cheered up, not to live totally in the past. You have the ability to utilise many genres of music, so mix it up if it is appreciated.

Legalities of Music

We are very lucky that we have the whole world of music available to us like never before. It is important that we support the artists that generate the music for us. Without them, line dancing wouldn't exist. We have the opportunity to ensure that the music we use is done so legally. All music should be purchased legally of course, but we also need to pay a licence fee, to use that music in public. Often there are two licence fees, one for the artist that creates the music, and one for the composer who writes the music.

The difficulty with this, is that less reputable instructors, who don't do things legally, have fewer costs, and so can charge less than the professionals. I can only encourage the dancers to support the instructors that do the right thing, to keep our industry and the music industry we live off, alive and professional.

Latin Rhythms and Line Dancing

In ballroom dancing, there are two ways of teaching the timing of the Latin rhythms of Cha-Cha and Rumba. I call them the Social Style and the Latin Style. They can both be done to the same music, which is Common Time, or a syncopated derivative of that.

Latin Rumba is Counted Hold, 2,3,4. Social Rumba is counted 1,2,3, Hold. So the Rumba movement starts on count 2 for Latin Rumba and on count 1 for Social Rumba.

Latin Cha-Cha is counted 1,2,3,4&. Social Cha-Cha is counted 1,2,3&4. So the Cha Movement starts on count 2 for Latin Cha Cha and count 1 for social Cha Cha.

These issues don't affect the terminology of the clusters, or the timing of the clusters, but it does affect the phrasing of the clusters to the beat of the music. It gives the "Latin timing" movements a different "feel" compared to doing them in "Social timing". The general line dancers find Latin timing much harder to do than Social timing. They may also tend to drift off the correct timing and into social timing if you are not vigilant.

"Samba" is also a Latin rhythm that has been absorbed into line dancing to some degree. However it has not been properly understood. The general timing for ballroom Samba is 1a2 (the middle move is delayed slightly), whereas many untrained line dancers think it is 1&2. Though this is a subtle difference, it does change the feel of the movements, and is only obvious with specific Samba music, rather than the more standard time music used in most line dancing.

Ear Worms

An Ear Worm sounds like a horrible disease or critter. For some people it might be. An Ear Worm is a song that you can't get out of your head. Some songs just won't go away. The name comes from a variation of a German word "Ohrwurm".

From Wikipedia: According to research by James Kellaris, 98% of individuals experience earworms. Women and men experience the phenomenon equally often, but earworms tend to last longer for women and irritate them more. Kellaris produced statistics suggesting that songs with lyrics may account for 73.7% of earworms, the rest due to instrumentals.

If a choreographer connects a dance to an "Ear Worm" song then it is likely to be a memorable dance. Some dance examples are: EZ Waltz (Lam) to Christy Lane's song: "Shake Me I Rattle", and Heidi (Wyllie) to Kurt Darren's song: "Heidi".

Changing the Music Speed

Quite often the original music speed is too fast for the first time attempting a dance. This can be solved in two ways.

Firstly you can find a different piece of music that is a more reasonable speed and try it to that, before moving on to the proper music. This helps make the dancers more adaptable. The down side is that the slower music is unlikely to have the phrasing of the original music, so you can't practice any interruptions.

The second solution is to use a music source with the option to change the speed of the music. If you have this, then I find slowing the music between seven and ten percent is the most useful amount.

If you do use a slower speed, you may want to only use part of it and move on. If you are going to cut the music, wait till a sequence is complete, and preferably when the dancers are facing the front, so they know it is deliberate. Fade the music out, rather than just stopping it abruptly. It is more professional.

Often you will be asked "is the music fast or slow?" This is a difficult question to answer, as each dance can have lots of 'holds' in it, enabling it to be done to fast music, or can use high levels of syncopation to make slow music more tolerable. Most dancers have no concept of beats per minute, so telling them that it is 124 bpm means nothing to them. Some instructors and dancers have invented their own, fairly humorous, measuring scale of music speed. I have heard the following expressions used to describe music speed:

- Super Slow
- Slow Slow
- Crazy Fast
- Real Slow
- Fairly Fast

For example, "No, it's not slow slow, but it is fairly slow"

Presentation

Your Time Management

It is important that you provide the dancers the maximum amount of activity they can fit into the session they are paying for. Make sure you are prepared to start before the clock ticks over. Make sure you consider how to finish the class on time, fifteen minutes before the end of the class, so you don't end up with time left over, but not enough to do another dance.

Make sure your watch is the correct time, and any clocks that are in your dance hall are also of the correct time. Don't forget about daylight savings if it happens in your area, and warn them the week before when it changes.

Think about inefficiencies that might be taking up your valuable teaching time. If you need glasses to see your sheet, don't leave them on the desk, then having to keep getting them to see. Put them on a chain around your neck. If you sweat a lot, have a small towel on your hip.

If you find a specific cluster hard, or time consuming to teach, find another more efficient way. If you can't think of one, ask a mentor for suggestions.

If you are having a break, tell them so they can take advantage. If you are not, then reduce the "dead space" between dance teaches to zero. Have whatever resources such as music and dance sheet ready at the start of the session, rather than waiting till you need it. That way you can go immediately into the next teach or walk through. Alternatively, while the dancers are completing the current dance, you should be preparing the material for the next teach. Have the music lined up and the sheet prepared, so you can flow on with the next teach, without having the dancers standing around getting bored.

Your Nerves

Almost everyone gets nervous when put into an unfamiliar situation. This tends to make them tense up and make mistakes that they would otherwise never do. It is important that you are aware of your state of tension, and attempt to relax somehow, to avoid these mistakes.

These situations may be:
- A visiting instructor walks into your class unexpectedly
- A stranger with unknown abilities comes to your class
- An experienced dancer comes to a beginners class
- A known trouble maker turns up at your class

When we are stressed, our muscles tighten up and our breathing changes and becomes shallow. As you breathe more lightly, you are participating in a vicious circle, because your body responds to your change in breathing with a fight-or-flight response, adding to your tension and stress.

A well-publicised relaxation technique is to imagine everyone in the room is naked. This may be more traumatic for you than the existing circumstances, but if it works give it a try. This is called visualisation. Take yourself to a "happy place".

A more likely effective exercise is to stop and take some deep even slow breaths. Just try to relax your breathing.

Most of all realise that you are the teacher, you are in charge, and you set the rules. Do not assume they are there necessarily to disrupt, they may be there to enjoy themselves. If not, kick them out.

Your Voice

Your voice is your most important asset as an instructor. It is important to look after it. If you don't use some form of electronic amplification you are likely to strain it. This could lead to nodules on your vocal chords and throat operations if you are not vigilant.

It is not necessarily volume of voice that is important, but clarity of speech. Learn to pronounce your words clearly, without clipping the endings as some lazy speakers tend to do. Speak slowly so people can actually understand every word. Often seeing a singing or public speaking coach is worthwhile to teach you these skills.

Loss of voice is often due to letting your throat dry out from too much air being expelled at a time. A simple exercise that will teach you to conserve your air is as follows:

Take a deep breath. Then start counting slowly every second without taking an additional breath, out loud. See what number you get to. A good public speaker should be able to get to at least thirty and still be heard clearly. Often when people try this the first time, they only get to about fifteen. It is something to practice. Make it a game with some of your friends.

How you speak is also important if you wish to keep the attention of your class. If you communicate in a monotone voice, you will put them to sleep. Try to keep some lilt in your voice with some ups and downs in tone. It is also important to keep your voice friendly, rather than overly commanding.

Having water to sip on during class is important to keep the vocal chords and throat lubricated. Usually tepid water is best, as too hot or too cold water may have a more dramatic effect on the voice or throat.

Don't forget, when people get nervous, they often speed up their speech, or say way too much. Try to speak slowly and clearly, especially when nervous.

Most important, don't forget to breathe. Many people get so caught up in trying to get as many helpful words out, that they forget to take a breath. If you can't find a place to breathe then you are probably walking the dance through too fast anyway.

If you miss a word, while taking a breath, don't try to catch up. Just move onto the next one. Try not to make the breath taking at a critical point. At the end of a count in, or just when you need to announce an interruption is not a good time for a breath gap, as it will cause dancer hesitation.

Your Diplomacy / MC Duties

When starting a class, welcome everyone, especially any new people. It is wise to learn the names of any new people before starting the class, in case you need to speak to them. This only works with little classes however (or instructors with amazing memories).

Make any announcements during the breaks. Acknowledging birthdays can go down well, but some classes don't like it, so be careful. Often there may be group discussions about news items of interest. Talking about sports is fine, but do try to avoid giving opinions about politics or religion. All you do is polarise the customers, and you are bound to offend someone.

Occasionally you will be asked to address awkward and uncomfortable situations. Sometimes a dancer will turn up with a high level of body odour, and will need to be spoken to. Sometimes disruptive dancers will need to be asked to "tone it down" for the sake of the other dancers. If you are conducting the class, it is your responsibility to handle these issues sensitively, and discretely.

When concluding a class, thank everyone for coming, and individually thank anyone who specifically helped out in some way.

Building and Maintaining Rapport with Dancers

A lot of dancers go to a particular venue because they like the instructor; or rather they like the instructor's style and approach. For this reason it is important to build a relationship with your dancers. The structure of that relationship is an individual thing and will be different for each instructor. However, there are some general points you can be aware of which will help you to build the "right" relationship.

The first and most important of these is that you must always be yourself. You cannot maintain a false front constantly, so don't make a rod for your own back by pretending to be someone you're not.

Another important point is to keep your personal life exactly that. Everyone has bad days and that's fine, but don't ever burden your dancers with something that doesn't concern them. Always be positive and bright when you are speaking with them, whether it's one on one, or with the whole class.

Always make yourself available to your dancers during classes. Treat every question and request with respect and try to give them the information they are looking for. If you can't help them on the spot, make a note of the problem, and tell the dancer/s you'll let them know. Then make sure you do follow through. It may be wise to ensure you have a paper and pen available to jot down any reminders you may need to make to collect requested information to bring to the following class.

Don't try to be a comedian. If you are naturally a "clown" that's fine, but don't overdo it. Never tell jokes, unless you are an expert at telling them (and most of us aren't). You can entertain the class with any funny stories about things that have happened to you. It is important to keep the stories brief however as the economists will not want their dancing time wasted. Be careful that you are the brunt of any misfortune, rather than someone in the class that may be embarrassed. This will cause lots of laughter and put the class at ease.

If you are taking the class for the first time, introduce yourself before you do anything else. If you have been teaching other classes, tell the dancers how long you've been teaching, If it's your very first class, SAY NOTHING.

FOR THE INSTRUCTOR

You'll be nervous enough without advertising the fact that you've never taught a class before.

Whether it's your first class, or your hundredth, it always pays to welcome the dancers at the door when you have the opportunity. They appreciate the personal contact and will respect you for it.

Acknowledge anyone who speaks to you from the floor. For example, if someone calls out a comment during your teach don't ignore them. People who do this are attention-seekers and if you ignore them they may well become disruptive. Sometimes it is fun feedback, and that can enhance the class and should be encouraged. Just don't let it take too much time from the main task of teaching. Not getting any feedback at all is worse, so don't suppress it.

Likewise, if someone asks you for further explanation on something give the further explanation to the whole class, and then check with the person who asked if you have helped them. Don't single them out by standing next to them and excluding everyone else, they may find this embarrassing.

Try to speak to any new people one on one during the breaks or after the class. Reassure them that it will take a few weeks before they start to make sense of what they are learning. Ask them to let you know if they are having problems. Your dancers should always feel comfortable about asking for help. Finding the best blend of teacher and friend is not easy, especially when you know that everyone is looking for a different mix. Some people respond best to authority, others respond better to friendly cajoling.

You will find what works best for your dancers over a period of time but use these hints as a general guideline. For the majority of dancers the class is a social outing and they don't want to be treated like school children (even if they are acting like it!). They want to have fun as much as they want to learn to dance, so please don't suppress this element of the class. For many people this is just a leisure activity and if they aren't having fun, then they may not continue coming along.

Your Diction and Language

Most countries and regions have local words and expressions. These are what make you unique. However use of them in a teaching environment may not work effectively, especially if you have a multicultural customer base, or teach outside of your area.

The use of expressions like: "yooze guys", "show ya", or "gunna go" are probably to be avoided.

Be polite when directing the dancers during the teaching of the dance. Pleases and Thankyous are still important. "Turn to the Front Please" is less abrupt and offensive than "Turn Around".

Understanding the correct pronunciation of moves and clusters is also important. I have heard "Kick Ball Chain" used many times, highlighting the speaker does not understand the meaning of the movement "Ball Change".

It is also important to try to limit the use of overloaded or confusing words. The expressions "go back to the front", or "step on your left foot" are not clear explanations, and could be easily misunderstood or misinterpreted, sometimes with humorous consequences.

It is also important to make your explanations as precise as possible. The expression: "We will be facing the back when we do the move" is not accurate. Rather it is: "We will be facing the back after we do the move". It seems fussy, but it is best to get into good habits from the start to make it as easy as possible for the dancers to get it right first time.

You may find relating real life experiences to teaching a movement helps get the message across. For example when teaching a drag, you could relate it to having chewing gum on your heel and you are trying to remove it as you drag the foot back. Or doing a Dig is like pushing a spade into the ground with your heel.

Some favourite quotes heard while training an instructor are:
- "Turn to your back, that will be your front there"

- "Face the back, we will try it from this side"
- "Point right heel forward" (how do you point a heel?)
- "We will be facing the back when we do it (will be facing the back AFTER we do it)
- "We will take it from the cross points" (does that mean before or after the cross points?)

Do not ask general questions of the dancers that will give up control of your programme or teaching techniques. You need to assess the situations yourself.

If you ask general questions "have you got that?" or "do you want it again?", some quick learner will give you an answer that will intimidate the slower dancers from replying. It is safer to ask: "Does anyone need that again?", or "Does anyone want that slower?" They are better structured questions that will allow the correct people to respond. It is the ones that don't reply that you are usually looking for an answer from.

Your Other Senses

As an instructor, you spend a lot of time with your back to your audience. This makes it a challenge to see what is going on behind you.

Many good instructors are accused of having eyes in the back of their heads. These instructors have developed good peripheral vision, requiring only a slight turn of the head to see directly behind them. They also develop fine-tuned hearing, being able to detect small steps or noises, not in time with all of the expected steps or noises.

Reading the Floor

This is more than just observing the body language of the individuals. It is important to get a feel for the overall mood of the dancers as the class progresses. It will change as the dancers get tired or "brain dead". Some of the causes may be:
- Saturation – You may get to a point in the class where their brains are saturated, and if you don't drop the level, you will lose dancers.

- Boredom – If you don't add something to spice the class up, or move on from the topic of discussion, they will lynch you.
- Dislike – If when you announce a dance to be done, and half the class sits down, then you have a problem. It may be because the dance is too hard, or has been done too often. Either way you would have to have a good reason to continue with it.

You may also notice that some people will develop a mind block about a particular part of a dance. You need to watch closely the steps leading up to their problem spot. It is likely that the preparation into the step is not right, rather than the actual step itself.

Reading the floor is vital when you teach a dance for the first time. Take note of any problems the dancers are having. If there is a consistent problem spot, then there is a good chance most dancers will have the same problem spot. Perhaps you can work out a training exercise for this particular part, and then the next time you teach the dance, you can overcome the problem more quickly.

Reading the floor will also tell you another vital piece of information - "Are my dancers enjoying themselves?" Watch their faces as well as their feet. Remember, enjoyment is a big part of line dancing. If there seems to be a downcast attitude amongst the dancers, try to find out why. Is the dance too hard? Are they too hot? Have you taught the dance thoroughly enough?

Another thing you will find out from reading the floor is the structure of the class, i.e. who are the leaders, who are the followers, who are the strongest dancers, who are the weakest? Knowing all these things will help you to better manage your class and to help all your dancers get the most out of their line dancing. It will also help you become a better instructor by giving you a measuring stick for self-evaluation. Take a few minutes after each class to evaluate your own performance. What problems did you have? How can you overcome them? Should you have done more preparation? Do you need to ask a mentor for some helpful hints?

Remember, there is always something you can do to improve your performance. Take the time after each class to be your own critic. It is an important part of your overall development as an instructor.

Your Feet

Many Instructors and dancers develop issues with their feet. Heel spurs, Plantar Fasciitis and tendon cysts are common. These can have many causes, but early detection and treatment is important. There are non-invasive alternatives to injections, operations and expensive orthotics. Explore them all if you have an issue.

Correct footwear and appropriate dance floors will minimise the issues, but many are caused by events earlier in life, and exacerbated by the dancing.

Your Clothing

People like to dress up when they go out. But they don't want to overdress and look silly. The person running an event should be the most overdressed person at the event. The saying goes "Dress to Impress". You cannot expect the dancers to dress up, if the guest or instructor doesn't.

If running a regular class, it is a good idea to have a "club" uniform. Usually a shirt of some sort, it gives the regulars an outfit that they can grab so they don't have to decide what to wear each week. This will also help with advertising and any performances you might do in public. Don't forget to remind new dancers that, just because someone is wearing a uniform, it does not automatically mean that they are skilled dancers.

For special events, it is nice to encourage a dressier atmosphere by dressing up yourself. It needn't be the traditional cowboy/country gear, but torn jeans and singlets do not say "professional" in my book, no matter how trendy it might seem to the wearer.

Positioning your Dancers

It is important to learn early on who your stronger dancers are, and who your weaker ones are. Before they get entrenched into a specific place on the floor of their choosing, it can be useful to allocate them a position.

If you have a few competent dancers, ideally put them in each corner of the dance floor to give the other dancers someone to watch, to reinforce the steps. If you only have one competent dancer, then put them down the back. But only do this if the dancer is reliable. It is your reputation that they are representing.

The most difficult places to dance are the corners. People dancing in the corners have no one to watch in front of them for half the time. People on an edge have no one to watch for a quarter of the time. People in the middle have always got someone to watch.

In a class situation, your newest, or weakest dancers should ideally be somewhere in the middle. Your strongest dancers should be in the corners. Your very strongest dancers should be in the back corners furthest from the instructor.

Over time, new people join the class, and existing dancers retire for whatever reasons. You may need to do a reshuffle of positions every once in a while. This may not be a pleasant task, as many people get very attached to their "spot". It is necessary if you want the class to learn as efficiently as possible. Often it will pay to speak to your target "experienced dancers" to prime them for the role you want them for.

Your Assistants

Most instructors have a small band of loyal assistants, or maybe just one of them. If there is more than one instructor teaching, it should be clear who is in charge at any one stage and anyone else stays silent.

It is great to have someone to take the money at the door and keep attendance records. This gives someone to greet people, introduce newcomers and handle issues, while the instructor is preparing the equipment or programme. As the instructor it is still important to keep a hand in at the door, which will help with remembering the names of your customers.

You also need to make it clear to them that there is only one instructor teaching at any time. They are not to verbalise instructions at the same time that you, the instructor, are teaching. Nor are they to question or argue with the instructor. If there is an issue, they should approach the instructor discretely and quietly to allow the instructor to correct or deal with the issue.

If there is to be any individual special tuition, by another person, it should be off the floor, and preferably in another room. This is not recommended, unless a deliberate parallel session is arranged as a feeder in an adjacent room.

Create a Demonstration Team

Many dancers (but not all) like to show off what they have learned. Putting together a demonstration team is one way to keep them involved. They have a feeling of belonging to the group and that social interaction is very important. It also provides you with another form of advertising when the opportunities arise. They really love to strut their stuff. Just be careful not to make it too serious that it generates its own problems and frictions. Make sure you are in charge, rather than passing that responsibility to someone else. It will only cause a power struggle that you don't need.

Warm Up and Cool Down Stretching

It is often proposed by those from the fitness industry, that have come into line dancing, that we should be having a stretching session prior to dancing. They also propose a stretching session after the dancing as well. The purpose of these warm up and cool down sessions is to prepare the muscles for the workout to avoid damage caused by sudden exertion.

In reality, this is not practical with line dancing, nor really needed. Most dances in class will be walked through before the music is put on. This will introduce the muscles to the forthcoming actions in a low stress manner anyway.

Most dancers want to dance, and respond with: "I didn't pay for an aerobics class. I paid for line dancing lessons".

If you want to use dancing time with aerobic stretches, that is your choice. The dancers will decide with their feet and may not return if they don't think they are getting value for money.

Background Music

It is often a good idea to have background music running softly as dancers arrive. This creates a little noise and atmosphere, rather than having them walking in to a silent clinical environment. Music reduces stress, which is why there is music in elevators.

Background music is also a great measuring stick for breaks. Most songs are around three minutes long. So put background music on during the breaks as well. Never have a break for longer than three songs, no matter what the topic of discussion might be. It is a dance class, not a discussion group.

When selecting the background music, try to use music that does not have a dance to it. Otherwise some smart-aleck will get up and try to dance to it, totally defeating the point of the break.

Video Recording

Occasionally a dancer may ask to video some or all of the class (sometimes they don't ask). You need to be aware of the issues involved in agreeing to the request. There is privacy, as well as music licencing issues involved in this situation. Those dancers being videoed should be made aware and be asked to agree to being recorded. Sometimes the person doing the recording is planning on using it for practice at home, but in the process misses the actual teach by holding the camera. Not ideal if they intend to dance it immediately with the rest of the class.

You should try to insure that the recording is not going to be used commercially, or be put on the internet, if your music is on the recording. You are licensed to play the music, but not to replicate the music.

Compensation for your Work

Teaching line dancing does require time and money to do properly. It seems fair that you should be compensated for that. Teaching a regular class requires a high level of commitment. Even if you are sick or just plain tired, if you treat your teaching professionally, the class must go on.

The dancers on the other hand rarely have the same level of dedication and commitment. If it's too hot, too cold, not feeling very well, had a funeral, babysitting the grandkids, on holidays, and the reasons go on, they don't have to turn up.

This leaves you with a dilemma. How do you charge a fee for your classes that guarantees you don't lose money at some stage. There are a few different options that you can consider.

The general method is charging at the door a set fee for each class, collected when they attend. This does not protect you from the whims of the dancers, weather and holidays, but it is easy to manage.

You can encourage regularity by having a "frequent dancer" accreditation that gives them a small discount if they attend multiple weekly classes over a set period of time, or attend regularly for a long period of time. This accreditation is lost if they don't maintain the commitment.

An alternative is to have a set monthly or annual charge that is paid prior to the class. This means people pay whether they turn up or not. It can be set up with swipe cards and regular credit card payments, but it is a lot of book keeping and equipment to set up and maintain. Most instructors can't be bothered with this and just wear the risk week by week.

The best attitude is to keep them wanting to return by providing the best service possible, to convince them that they are getting value for their money.

Sound Equipment

While a class is small, many instructors just use a "boom box" and their voice to run their classes. For the professionals however, some form of voice projection and music amplification is essential.

The main component parts are: Music Source, Amplifier, Mixer, Cordless Microphone and Speaker

Many of these parts can be purchased as combined units, depending on how much volume and how large an area is needed to be covered.

Amplification

Most guitar amplifiers are robust, so they won't break easily while being transported, and they have sufficient mixing ability to take both a music source and a microphone input. They are suitable for a small hall of up to thirty or so dancers and they have a solid speaker built in.

Mixer

It is wise to have some control over treble (high frequency) and bass (low frequency) tone, preferably with separate voice and music controls. This will allow the sharpness of some songs to be reduced, and the clarity and projection of the voice to be improved. If your voice sounds muffled, turn up the treble and turn down the bass. If the music is shrill and piercing, turn down the treble and turn up the bass.

If a dancer complains that the music is too loud, they often mean it is too shrill. Try just reducing the treble, rather than the volume.

The mixer needs to be able to control the microphone volume at the same time as the music is playing. Some combined amplifiers with built in mixers automatically drop the music volume when the voice through the microphone is detected. This is fine for speeches at a wedding, but is disastrous for dance teaching.

You must be able to be heard clearly over the music. Don't be intimidated by the shushers. The volume of the music creates atmosphere. They also need to be able to hear it down the back. Keep monitoring and adjusting the voice and music balance if there are issues.

Microphone

A good cordless microphone is essential for professional teaching. Usually a head worn microphone, as a hand held microphone gets in the way of arm actions such as clapping and clicking etc.

The main issue with cordless microphones is that they use public radio frequencies to operate, and the availability of these frequencies is regulated by government. Governments have the habit of reallocating frequency spectrums to television and radio, causing equipment to be illegal and non-functional. Ideally this will be fixed with BlueTooth streaming microphones in the near future.

If you use a hand held microphone, rest the edge of the microphone just below the lower lip on the chin. Keep it in contact with the skin. That way if you turn your head the microphone will go with it. If you have a head microphone, make sure the microphone is near the corner of the mouth. By keeping the distance consistent with the mouth, the volume will be stable and the voice as clear as possible.

Either microphone should have a wind guard on them to stop the breathing noises coming through the speakers.

Music Source

No matter what I put here, it will be out of date shortly. I started my dance teaching using vinyl records, moved on to cassettes, then CD's, then MiniDiscs all in 20 years. At the time of printing this book, I use a laptop with mp3's of the music required.

Whatever system is used, it should enable some variations in the music being played. You need the ability to change the tempo (speed) of the music without changing the tone. Ideally you need to be able to set a jump into the music, and fade the end if required.

It is important to have an easy to use, easy to find filing system for your music. The last thing you need is to waste time searching for a particular song. We have developed our own in house line dance DJ software to give us the simplicity we need for technically challenged instructors as well as the power for those needing to cope with more demanding situations.

Maybe in the future we will have "Heads-Up Displays" on all the dancers, or embedded chips in the clothing or shoes with all the dances programmed. Technology could take us anywhere. Isn't it exciting?

Research and Training

In any field of endeavour, it is important to keep up to date with the industry. Line dancing is no different. There are magazines, blogs, online chat groups and associations that you can join or subscribe to.

Before you hand over good money to them, try to ensure you are actually going to receive some benefit from the investment.

Information you should be looking for are:
- Cheaper Insurance
- Cheaper Licencing
- Current popular dances
- Instructor training sessions
- Equipment, Music and computer software advice
- Advertising and promotion opportunities
- Regional Workshop information
- General line dance related gossip

Organisational Memberships

Make sure any association you become a member of has line dancing as its primary focus, rather than an organisation that is an umbrella for many dance forms. These umbrella organisations sometimes are looking for fee paying members, rather than the best interest of line dancing, and often don't understand the specific needs of line dance.

Line dancing is a very unique dance form, and breaks many of the structural rules and assumptions made by other dance industries.

Also make sure that your membership is used for the development of the local industry, rather than just in supporting national bureaucracy, or regional activities and competitions.

Accreditation

In many industries, accreditation is used by trainers to provide a set of standards in content and methodology, to measure each other by. They can then use that accreditation in their advertising to promote their importance and knowledge. When an industry is very competitive, this can give some people a publicity and recognition edge over others with less or no accreditation.

Until there is a world-wide standard of terminology, dance sheet and teaching techniques, any accreditation system for line dancing will be very local in content, and potentially not very useful. At this stage, the line dance industry is not professional enough for this to have any impact. Hopefully in the future it will.

Beginner line dancers generally do not know what makes a good instructor, and what does not. Being a member of organisation ABCD, or having won competition EFGH means very little to any of them, impressive as it might seem to you.

Training and Self Development

If you intend to become an instructor, it is wise to find an experienced instructor to take you on as an apprentice. They will be able to show you the techniques that work for them, and to critique your methods as you develop.

If there is no-one in your area willing to take you on, you might find someone you respect in another area, and get some training from them remotely. This could be done using video clips from a tablet or phone.

Otherwise you might contact the local line dance association to find out what training programmes they have in place.

In our organisation, we take on apprentices for about six to nine months before giving them a beginner's class of their own. When they are ready to teach the next level up, we give them an additional six months of training.

We train them in existing classes, getting them to progressively teach more and more of the class each week, till they are running the complete class. During that time we provide written critique of their performance, which is discussed, in private, after the class. When they are ready, another instructor, other than the one training them, will provide a final authorisation.

We also run instructor workshops, every ten weeks, for our existing instructors to network and share experiences and suggestions.

If you want to be a good instructor, you need to be able to take criticism and modify your behaviours to suit. If you want to be a good trainer, you need to learn how to give critique without destroying confidence.

Remember, you can learn what to do from good instructors, and what not to do from bad ones.

Keeping your Suppliers Happy

The existence of your class and your income is based on the work of others as well. You are only one link in the dance food chain. Other people are also trying to make a living in the dance/music industry, and it is in your best interest to support them where possible.

Some of these suppliers are:
- Venue Owners
- Musicians
- Composers
- Dance Website Developers
- Choreographers
- DJ Software Developers
- Dance Sheet Proof Readers

This support may be by subscription or licensing, verbal promotion, or cash donation. Either way they should be encouraged and supported to continue doing their good work.

Advertising and Promotion

Advertising is very important when starting a new class. Once a class is established, there is still need to provide a steady stream of new dancers to replace dancers who leave for various reasons.

There are many people and organisations out there that are willing to take your money to promote your product. Most of them are a waste of money, but you need to consider the benefits and return on investment for each. Know who your prospective customers are, and select a medium that will get to them best.

I have found over the years that the best form of advertising is public demonstrations and word of mouth promotion. There is minimal cost in both of these methods. Having a clear simple hand out sheet available to your dancers, to pass on to friends and acquaintances, is important.

Local radio can be an important media. Sometimes radio based community announcements and "come 'n' try" promotions are free. You can also regularly scour local brochures and magazines for possible demonstration opportunities. Be aware that there are also many organisations that would appreciate and enjoy a performance of line dancing, but not all of them will lead to potential recruits for the classes. You may need to be selective, or risk burning out your performance team with little benefit to your class.

Many people suggest having a first class free policy. I hate running a class with a group of beginners that turn up for one week only and then never return, without even paying for your efforts. It is also disruptive to the rest of the class to have to drop back to fundamentals, knowing that the freebies are not likely to return.

I recommend a variant on a free class for beginners. If an existing dancer brings a new person, the existing dancer gets their class for free that week.

You will be working hard on the new beginner, so should get some return on that work. However you are then encouraging your experienced dancers to promote your class and rewarding them for it.

If you want to experiment with a free class concept, I recommend running specific "come 'n' try" sessions, so you get all of the newbies at the same time. They then may form friendships with other newbies that may encourage them to return to meet up again. Existing dancers can be encouraged to "bring a friend" for those sessions.

Getting the people into the class is the hardest part, but keeping them is even more important. Find out their expectations early and try to deliver them quickly.

I Hate that Dance!

How many times have you heard that, as an instructor? It often means "I can't do that dance!" I never believe the person till I've seen them actually accomplish the dance. Often it is too hard, or is to music they don't like. However I have seen dances that people "hate" becoming their favourites once they have "got it".

Some people dislike waltzes. I recommend that you do not programme multiple waltzes in a row in class or at socials. Break them up with other rhythm dances. In reality, try to keep dances of similar rhythms apart, just to increase the variety of the dancing experience.

I Hate That Song!

People's tastes in music are very diverse. I have dancers that hate twangy country music; I have dancers that hate ABBA. I have dancers that hate risqué lyrics. Most people will tolerate music they don't like because the next one is bound to be better. If you provide a diverse music selection and mix it up, this is usually the case.

People's reactions to a song they dislike can however be very diverse and disruptive. We have had a dancer drop to the floor and kick the legs in the air till it stops. Most just walk out till the song is over. Just be prepared to handle it if it happens and keep it in mind for future reference and don't pander to these people.

Line Dance Instructor Competencies

For a person to be a competent instructor, they should be able to demonstrate the following skills:

- Be a competent line dancer
- Be able to "count in" multiple types of music introductions
- Be able to teach pulse and rhythm to non-dancers
- Demonstrate beat cuing without music
- Be able to cue at a constant tempo at a minimum of three different tempos
- Be able to explain action, move and cluster terminology
- Demonstrate beat and pre-emptive cueing with music
- Be able to correctly interpret multiple dance sheets
- Be able to accurately determine the level of a dance sheet without relying on the choreographers level evaluation
- Be able to effectively set up and control their sound system
- Be able to evaluate hazards in a dance venue and remove them
- Be able to recognise dancer's execution issues and be able to recommend appropriate corrections
- Be able to explain a cluster and/or action in multiple ways
- Be able to recognise potential hazards in a dance's choreography and recommend alternatives to avoid those hazards
- Be able to chunk a dance efficiently for easiest teaching to dancers
- Be able to reassemble chunks efficiently for easiest teaching to dancers
- Be able to plan and execute a full class session programme

For the person to be considered a good instructor they should also have the following attributes (not necessarily in this order):

- Patience
- Personality
- Good diction and enunciation
- Tolerance
- Enthusiasm
- Diplomacy
- Tactfulness
- Empathy
- Pleasant voice
- Not Patronising
- Sense of humour
- Not too serious
- Approachable
- Well prepared
- Flexible in teaching technique
- Precision in footwork
- Clarity and efficiency of description

Your First Class

If you are about to run your first class, there is a checklist of things you would be wise to run through.

Check out your new venue. Make sure you know things like:

- Do I have the key?
- Which door do I use?
- Where is the power point?
- Where are the light switches?
- Where are the toilets and do they need a key?
- Where can I park?

FOR THE INSTRUCTOR

- Where can the dancers park?
- Is there a public phone, or access to a phone? (If you don't have a working cell phone for emergencies)
- How long will it take me to get to the venue?
- Where are the chairs for the dancers?
- Is there a table for the sound equipment?
- What are the instructions for the heaters, fans, air conditioners and kitchen appliances if needed?

Make sure you have set up and used your sound equipment at home a number of times prior to your first class. Don't leave it till your class to find out something is not working.

Organise someone reliable and friendly to be your door person for the first night. It is nice to have someone to share the nerves and reduce the anxiety with. Arrive at your class early enough to have plenty of time to set up, but not too early. This would just give you more time to worry.

Just remember, teaching a dance is a very different situation than just dancing it. So be well prepared with the material you intend to use, and be flexible enough to change if it is not working.

At the end of the class thank the dancers and the door person. Then, if possible, stand by the door as they leave, as they will want to ask questions or make comments as they leave. It will be valuable feedback.

When you have packed everything up and left the venue, take the time to assess yourself. This is a valuable exercise you should do after every class as this will ensure your presentation is always of the highest possible standard.

FOR THE CELEBRITY OR WORKSHOP INSTRUCTOR

Many choreographers that have had success with their creations go "on the road" to become guest instructors at events and workshops nationally and internationally. Some of them have never actually taught a class, but are expected to know how to teach and entertain. This can be an exciting time for them, but also very daunting and lonely. Living out of hotel rooms, always on the run, can be draining.

Find Out your Customers Expectations and Experience

It is important to do as much research as possible about:
- Who you are going to teach?
- Where are they from?
- Are they from multiple groups, or from one teacher's classes?
- How long have they been dancing?
- What dances do they know?
- What language do they speak?
- What are their favourite music genres?

It is important to correspond with the local instructors that are providing the customers to ensure you know what their expectations are. If you don't meet these expectations, then you are unlikely to be invited back. You are also unlikely to get word of mouth referrals, which are essential to your ongoing popularity. You also need to know the event coordinators expectations. They are the one providing you the opportunity to perform. Look at the advertising material used to promote your workshop, so you can see what was promoted about you.

Quite often a workshop event will be combined with a social, or multiple socials. If as part of the ticketing there is a request component for the social, you can gauge the tastes of the customers by getting access to the request list (providing you recognise the dance names).

Gather your Material

Many instructors use these workshops to promote their own choreography. There are advantages in doing this. You can control when the dances have been released to the general public, allowing for exclusive first use of the material. It does mean you need a continuous stream of new material if you do multiple events.

Because of the amazing distribution speed of the line dance network, using social media and the internet, a new dance doesn't stay new and unknown for very long. If you recycle dances from previous workshops, you may find that many people already know the dances and will not consider they are getting value for money.

Some celebrity instructors have developed a network of non-celebrity choreographers that feed them with new unreleased or regionally popular dances. They can then pick and choose material that is appropriate for whatever crowd they are performing to, with little chance that the material is familiar to the dancers. This is advantageous to the non-celebrity choreographers, because they get exposure for their creations, which may in the future lead to them to get called up to do their own celebrity appearances.

Select your Material

Assuming that you have a wide selection of material to choose from, you then have to narrow down which dances you are going to teach, and how many will fit in to the time frame you have been given. It is wise to select a range of difficulties, and a range of music styles, with a few spares up your sleeve. If there is a step-sheet booklet that is to be printed, then your ability to be flexible is reduced. It will still be wise to have some spares to switch to if there are unexpected issues.

Some of the issues you may run into are:
- The music has already been used locally for another dance
- The dance has already been done in the area
- The dance is too hard for the customers
- The dance is too easy for the customers
- The customers don't approve of the style of music you are using
- The customers don't understand your language, accent or terminology

Choose the Order of Presentation

This assumes you are presenting more than one dance. The first dance you present will be at the easier end of the spectrum, and preferably a known winner. It is better to start easy and work up, calling it a warmup dance, than starting hard and blowing them away immediately. This also gives you the opportunity to gauge the ability of the floor, in order to appropriately select subsequent material.

You should also save an easier dance or two for the end of the session, in case you have a few minutes up your sleeve, or in case the dance you had planned on presenting will take too long, or is too hard for the customers.

It is better to teach a reasonable number of shorter, achievable dances, rather than one long, less attainable dance. By doing a selection of dances, the chances are much higher that you will give them at least one or two dances that they like, and will therefore take back to their home classes. If they only get one dance in a multi-hour session (which I have witnessed), then you only have one shot at capturing their favours.

Present the Material

Before getting out onto the stage to do your presentation, make sure you know the controls of the sound equipment being used. Make sure you know where the batteries for the microphone are, and the volume of the music. There may be a DJ to get to know, or you may be expected to do it yourself. If there is a DJ, set up a set of hand signals to inform the DJ of adjustments you may need to music and voice. This could mean speed control as well as volume.

If you have an assistant/partner at the event, have them monitoring the audience for any issues that may be arising, and check in with them between teaches to ensure that you are fully in control of the presentation. They are likely to see things before you do or issues that you miss.

Remember that, unlike your own dancers, these people have not heard you or been taught from you before. They will not be used to your diction, accent or sentence construction. Speak slower than you would normally, and be very clear in your explanations. Do not presume knowledge or experience. Do not rush the presentation due to time constraint, instead select more appropriate material. It is better to teach three dances well, than teach four dances rushed.

The way you present material at a workshop can be quite different from presenting at your own class. In a class situation, you are creating building blocks of knowledge and terminology for future use. In a workshop situation, you want to get the choreography across in the most efficient way possible. You may need to adopt local language and terminology where possible.

You may need to provide more visual demonstrations of what is required, rather than verbal descriptions to overcome language difficulties. This will often include a centre floor demonstration of the dance prior to teaching it, either on your own, or with anyone else that may already know the dance.

If the room is crowded, or if there is no stage, you may need to venture onto the floor at various places during the teach, to demonstrate tricky parts to people that cannot see through the crowd. This may involve doing the same thing at multiple places on the floor. Some presenters even rotate the rows of the audience forward every few minutes to give everyone an opportunity to view the stage. This is time consuming with a large audience, and I don't recommend it, but if it works for you, then do it.

Review the Material

It is important near the end of the presentation that you do a quick review of everything you have covered. This doesn't just take up time, but is also important to reinforce the learning. If you present too much material, they will get saturated, and won't remember anything.

Get Honest Feedback

Unless you get feedback from your presentation, you will not be able to improve your performance for your next event. It is wise to have a series of questions to ask of the event coordinator, and indeed to ask of some of the customers (in private, not over the microphone). When asking them, make it clear that you want honest feedback, not to just have your ego stroked. Structure the questions to get answers that take some thought and explanation, rather than simple yes or no answers.

Some important questions might be:
- Which of the dances are you planning on taking back home?
- Which dances didn't you like?
- Which music appealed most of all?
- Which music didn't go down as well?
- What could I have improved on in my presentation?

Make sure you have contact information in the form of a business card to distribute to any prospective event coordinators that might want your services. Each event opportunity is likely to be different, but you need to have a fair idea what remuneration you are expecting from the event.

Sometimes it may be just travel and accommodation expenses, other times you may require an appearance fee. Be up front and honest about your expectations, but flexible enough to cope with unforeseen circumstances outside the control of the event coordinator.

FOR THE LINE DANCE EVENT COORDINATOR

There are many different events that will attract line dancers. Some will even attract the general public. Each style of event has its own style of customers and its own issues.

Generally the biggest issue in keeping actual line dancers entertained is to give them as much floor time actually dancing as possible. They will watch stuff for a while, but eventually, want to get out and dance.

Socials

Whatever the size or purpose of the social, the most important decisions to make are the selection of the venue, DJ and sound equipment.

The venue needs to be large enough to accommodate the expected crowd, with sufficient refreshments and toilet facilities. It needs to have good acoustics and parking facilities for sufficient cars.

Many DJ's will come with sound equipment and music, but the equipment needs to be powerful enough to drive the selected venue. Make sure the DJ is familiar with the tastes and knowledge of the customers you are expecting to attract. It may pay to collect requests from potential customers, to give to the DJ, to give them an idea of what to expect.

The DJ needs access to a large array of music to cover requests, or be able to take in music from the attendees to satisfy their requests. If it is a set programme, then the DJ needs to have all the necessary music.

Local Socials

These events are usually run by a local instructor, primarily to supplement their own dancer's social activities. The coordinator knows the customers, knows their abilities, and knows their preferences. Often the programme for these events will be planned ahead of time, based on what has recently been done in the classes.

Regional Socials

These socials are usually put on by one of the major instructors in the area, or by a local line dancing organisation or state body. This usually requires the cooperation of most, if not all, of the line dancing groups in the area. It may also attract visiting dancers from outside the area or state if it is advertised widely enough.

Coordinating the playlist for the event can be challenging, with so many teachers involved, and therefore so many different dancers.

Quite often these will be annual events, and attract a regular group of attendees over time. They are usually based in the largest city of the region because of the accommodation and transport logistics.

National Conventions/Socials

These are bigger versions of the Regional Socials, but with even more diversity of customers. If these are set up, they generally rotate around the major population areas of the nation, so that one particular city or group does not dominate running the event. Otherwise ongoing communication and support may break down.

Themed Socials

If you want to run something different, then adding a theme to a social can be quite stimulating. There are many ways to do this, some requiring a lot of work from the organisers, some requiring work from the dancers.

The easiest is a dress up theme. It needs to be something that people can get costumes that are cheap and creative. Some examples are:
- Letter Theme – Come dressed as a word starting with a certain letter
- Era Theme – Seventies Disco, Fifties Rock & Roll etc.
- Location Theme – On the Farm, Nautical etc.

A more complex theme for the coordinator is a musical theme. This may require a lot of homework for the event DJ. With patience, you can find popular music from a specific era, or style, then you set current day dances to that music. You will find some amazing surprises, with a lot of work. You will also find there are already dances that you do, to some of that era music. This can make up the whole nights entertainment, or just a few feature brackets. Some suggestions are:
- Fifties Rock & Roll / Bobby Sox Ball
- Sixties Flower Power
- Seventies Disco
- Eighties Punk
- Christmas
- Country
- Bad Taste
- Retro
- Countries of the World

If you use a music theme, then the challenge is to find music that will fit some of the unusual rhythms that we now dance to. You can also team the music theme up with a costume theme for a full on effect.

Another popular theme for a social is a "Classics" social. This only works for line dance groups that have been dancing for a long time. Go back to what you were dancing ten years or more before, and check out the archives. This theme won't work with beginners as they don't have the dance history.

You can also set the difficulty level of a social. We find Easy Level socials are very popular, and a great introduction for the newer dancers, to the concept of socials. We have found Intermediate and Advanced only socials are not successful. The dancers burn out by half way through the social. They need the chill down time that the lower level dances provide, rather than all stress and challenge.

Workshops

Sometimes these are standalone events, and sometimes they are run as part of a competition or social. Either way, you will need to select presenters for the workshops, and set up a schedule of their presentations.

Selecting Presenters

Not all instructors make good workshop presenters. A workshop presenter needs to be one that will attract customers, entertain the customers, and then leave them wanting more. They need to have good diction and presentation skills, and access to appropriate material for your customers. They also need to have very good time management and observation skills.

Scheduling Presenters

When scheduling presentations, especially if there are multiple venues, you will need to allow time for the customers to get from one venue to the other. Ideally a workshop should be between one and one and a half hours, especially if there are multiple workshops in a row. Usually a ten minute gap is scheduled between workshops to allow people to get drinks, or change their position on the floor, or even move to another venue.

As the event coordinator, you need to meet with the DJ and the presenters to clearly state the expectations and responsibilities of each of them. It is important to clearly define the time schedule in order to minimise overruns between workshops. Clarify how many dances are being taught, and the appropriateness of those dances to the expected audience. Ideally this is

Reviewing Presenters and Workshop Overall

At the conclusion of the workshops, it is worthwhile taking a few notes on what worked and didn't work during the event. This will help recalling issues and dealing with them should you decide to run another event in the future. It will also enable you to give constructive feedback, should the presenters request it for their self-development.

Longest, Largest, Line Attempts

Over the years there have been many attempts at getting into the "Guinness Book of Records" for line dance related activities. Sometimes this type of presentation is just done to publicise a particular organisation (often charitable), or public event. I have participated in the opening of a new tunnel with line dancing from one end to the other, and also at the opening of a new river bridge with rows of dancers from end to end. Often country music festivals will have a longest line event as part of their publicity.

I have participated in an international line dance event where dancers in groups, all over the world, did the same dance at the same global time, to the same music. I have participated in events that have dancers around an oval at a sporting grand final. Many charities have used a longest line attempt as a fundraiser.

Whatever the purpose, the logistics of setting up such an event are actually very difficult. Most difficult is providing music to all the participants that may not be able to see each other, let alone hear a single music source. This is especially difficult outdoors. Music takes a while to travel distances, so keeping all the dancers in time with each other is very difficult.

To accomplish this will often require broadcast of the music to multiple receivers. It will also require a clear understanding of when the dancing will commence, and where everyone will be standing when they participate. There may also be a costume requirement, depending on the event. This costume may be sold at or before the event, or provided by the participants under guidelines for the event.

Even the logistics of publicity, registering and then counting the participants can be quite a mammoth undertaking. It can be lots of fun, when it is successful. It helps if there is some sort of souvenir of the event that is given or available for purchase at the event.

Competitions

Competition line dancing has become an important part of many people's line dance calendars. It gives them an opportunity to measure their abilities against others both locally and further afield. There are many different sizes of events, and each has their own style, focus, rules and challenges.

Regional Competitions

These can often be set up are training grounds for state, national and international events. Often to compete in a national event you must have competed at a regional level.

State, National or International Championships

These require enormous levels of cooperation between the organisers, and are usually run by national or state line dance organisations, or very experienced promoters.

Types of Competitions

Most competitions will have various age specific categories, as well as open categories for mixed age groups and general dancers. Sometimes they will also have teacher and student categories. Each will have specific eligibility requirements that need to be considered before entering.

Judging

It is wise to publicise the judging form, with the criteria used to determine the scores for each categories. Both the judges and the competitors need to be aware of the same rules, so there are few surprises, and disputes are minimised. Personal taste will always have some effect, but it should be minimised with clear criteria.

Judging should be by experienced practitioners that have no vested interests in the participants that they are judging. If they are teachers of, or friends with, any of the competitors, they should excuse themselves from judging that particular category.

If there are awards for overall best performances across all categories, then there needs to be a loading for the larger teams, over the smaller teams. There should also be a loading for the different age and experience categories to give them a fair shot at the overall award. Remember, the more in the group, the harder it is to get right, so the more impressive the performance.

Each competition will have its own set of criteria to describe what the coordinators consider to be important, however they are likely to include the following:

- Outfits – Neatness and clothing coordination of the team
- Entrance Routine – How the dancers make their way to the performance location
- Exit Routine – How the dancers make their way from the performance location?
- Start of the Dance – Do the team start the routine at the same time as each other?
- Unity of the Team – Do the team stay in synch with each other throughout the performance? Points will be lost for individual mistakes or lack of synchronisation between team members during turns etc. A space is left for making marks as mistakes are noticed or brief comments if required.
- Degree of Difficulty – Is the routine that the dancers are performing of high or low difficulty?
- Technique – Do the dancers execute the movements correctly? This may be according to the sheet, or according to appropriate dance

style depending on the criteria. Points will be lost if the dance isn't performed to the required choreography during the non-freestyle parts of the performance. Points will also be lost if the actions being undertaken are not sharp or precise, even though they may be performed in unison with the rest of the team.

- Finish of Dance – Do the dancers execute an appropriate and coordinated finish to the dance?
- Enthusiasm – Do the dancers look like they are enjoying themselves?
- Freestyle – If appropriate! If it is a freestyle category, points may be awarded for each unique freestyle addition to the original choreography. No extra points for repeat additions.

If it is a freestyle category, then there may be points for some criteria while executing the vanilla component and points for the same criteria in the freestyle component.

It may be appropriate to add to the application form something like the following paragraphs.

- As all entries are eligible for the overall trophies for top line dance and also top freestyle line dance, a system of handicap points are given to balance up the various categories against each other. These handicap points acknowledge that the more team members there are, the harder it is to coordinate and get correct. They also acknowledge that some age groups have a disadvantage in dexterity or experience and some balancing is required there as well.
- There will be five judges per category, with the top and bottom scores being discarded and the rest being totalled.
- The judges have been selected from volunteers representing many of the line dance teaching teams around the region, without any dominance by any organisation or club.

Venue and Performance Information

Competitors should be given every opportunity to create the best possible presentation for the event. This means giving them as much information as they can, for the coaches to prepare the participants properly. The participants and judges need to know ahead of time:

- What is the size of the dance area?
- Is the dance area elevated?
- Where are the entrances and exits from the dance floor?
- Where is the audience going to be, i.e. how many sides?
- Whether or not you are required to dance to the judges or the audience?
- What are the time restrictions?
- What are the music genre restrictions?
- Is music splicing eligible?
- How is the music to be provided?
- What are the styling restrictions, i.e. hat-work, arm-work etc.?
- Are there vanilla restrictions?
- Are there any styling restrictions during the vanillas?

Small Group Competitions

These competitions are for duos, trios or groups of less than a specified number of participants (13 for example). There is only one act on the dance floor at any one time.

Sometimes the dances that are to be presented are pre-selected, to enable clearer judging standards. Other times the dance can be selected by the participant, within the guidelines set out by the event. There may be a restriction on the genre of music, or the length of the presentation. In that case, often the presentation will be a splicing of a number of different dances, and possibly a number of different songs.

Large Group Competitions

These competitions are for large team presentations of participants (13 or more for example, but sometimes up to 50 or so). They are very spectacular to watch, and extremely difficult to manage as a coach. There is only one team on the floor at any one stage.

The presentation is usually limited in time. It is likely to be a splicing of different dances and different music over the presentation. The more complex the splicing, the more difficult it is to coordinate the presentation as a coach. Sometimes the large group may split into smaller groups, who then interact in formations with the other smaller split off groups, before recombining into a large formation again.

Not only does the dancing choreography need to be practiced and perfected, but the formation choreography also needs to be practiced and perfected.

Solo Competitions

Solo line dancing seems to be a miss-representation of the dance form. How can it be a line dance if there is only one person dancing in the "line". This form of competition does give the novice a place to start especially in the basic sections. It is also an opportunity for those that don't have a team or even a dance partner to participate in a competition. There are usually three or less competitors on the dance floor at any stage.

There are specific dances that the entrants must study and prepare for the event. They must dance the pre-selected dances, firstly "vanilla" for one or more sequences, and then they can add whatever variations and styling that they want that is within the rules of the event. Just remember, each competition may have its own different rules.

The intent is that they must stay true to the original traffic pattern of the dance, and not interfere with the other competitors that may be on the dance floor with them.

Choreography Competitions

Choreography competitions are intended to compare individual dance creations against each other. It is difficult however to remove the judging of the dance from the judging of the choreographer themselves. Many choreographers have reputations that they have cultivated over the years, and this may have an impact on how a dance is judged, if the rules are not carefully set up.

I have documented here a system that could be used to make a fair and interesting choreography competition. It assumes that dances submitted to the competition have not been released, nor have they been taught anywhere in the public arena. Any that had, would be disqualified from entering.

When the entries are accepted for the competition, they must be accompanied by the following information:

- 1 Original Dance Sheet – The sheet that would be available to the public
- 3 Anonymous Dance Sheets – Original Dance Sheet minus any choreographer's information or logos. There should not be any formatting that will indicate the choreographers identity either
- Names and contact information (phone and postal) of two competent dancers attending the competition that are willing to present a dance
- 3 USB sticks with an mp3 file of the music as the only file on each of them, with the name of the dance clearly marked

The event coordinator, upon receiving all of the entries, can redistribute an anonymous dance sheet and a music stick to each of the nominated dancers. This way it can be assured that no one is dancing their own dance, and the audience and the judges do not know who choreographed each dance till the award presentations.

Any issues with the dance sheets would have to be communicated through the coordinator, either during or prior to the event. All the scores would be tabulated prior to announcing the choreographers of the dance. It would mean a true representation of the interpretation of the dance sheet and a fairer distribution of the results.

The scores would be a summary of points given to encourage complete and accurate dance sheets, as well as a good dance. Points would be deducted for dance sheets that are resubmitted due to corrections prior to the event.

Sometimes there is a component of the competition for an overall winner across all the level categories. In this case, a loading factor would need to be added to the scores to acknowledge that the harder the dance is, the easier it is to make it interesting. Easier level dances get a higher bonus score than the hard level dances.

Points should be given for the following information on the original dance sheet:

- Choreographers Name, City/Town, State, Country
- Choreographers contact information. People cannot get information or interpretation on the sheet (or book the choreographer for workshops) if they cannot get in touch with them.
- Date of the creation of the dance
- Version number of the sheet. A version number allows updated/corrected sheets to be distinguished from the original outdated sheets, i.e. version 1 etc
- Number of Walls, Number of Beats, Proposed Level
- Target music title, artist, album
- Target music speed in bpm, length in min and sec
- Target music count in appropriately described
- No copying restrictions present. You don't want to restrict copyright if you want the sheet distributed

Points should be given for the appropriateness and usability of the music selected. For example have a total number of points for appropriateness, then subtract two points for every five seconds over four minutes, and subtract two points for every five seconds under two minutes and thirty seconds. Also subtract two points for every five seconds that the introduction music is over thirty seconds. If the music is too long it is boring, if the music is too short you don't really have the chance to enjoy the dance.

Points should be given for the accuracy of the choreography description on the dance sheet. There should not be an assessment of the head cue terminology. This terminology is based on education of the choreographer, rather than the dance itself, and should not be a assessment of the dance.

The detailed description however should be judged. Things that should be assessed are:

- Timing – Is the timing described in full
- Levelled – Is the choreography appropriate for the level specified
- Complete – Are the descriptions complete and easy to understand
- Neatness – Is the sheet neat, and does it contain any spelling errors
- Interruptions – Are the interruptions appropriately described and documented

Points should be given for the presentation on the dance floor. Remember you are judging the dance choreography, not the dancer's performance. Sometimes it is easier to assess the criteria by having a total and taking off points, rather than accumulating points, Things that should be assessed are:

- Rhythm – Does the choreography match the rhythm of the music used
- Mood – Does the choreography match the mood of the dance
- Music – Is the music appropriate for line dancing and pleasant to dance to
- Smoothness – Is the choreography smooth flowing
- Travel – Is the dance appropriately compact in its space requirements
- Turning – Are the turns comfortable and not overly turning in one direction
- Leggedness – Is the overall weight distribution comfortable
- Interruptions – Are the interruptions smooth to transition and easy to remember
- Visual – Is it a visually interesting dance appropriate to its level
- Appeal – Is it a dance you would like to learn appropriate to its level

It might also be interesting to include a component of the overall score from the actual two dancers that present the dance. They are the only ones that have actually practiced and prepared the dance and will no doubt have an opinion worth capturing. It also makes them feel valued.

However the points are allocated to these criteria, the judging sheet should be available with the entry form to the competition and the rules and judging criteria of the competition, long before submitting the entry. This ensures that there is a clear understanding of what you are expecting from your entrants and from the judges.

Correctly levelling the dance for a choreographer can be difficult. Especially, if there are level criteria for the competition. Often a true level of a dance can only be determined after it has been taught a few times to a typical dance class. If they teach the dance then it becomes ineligible for the competition, creating a problem. Therefor it is appropriate that an official guideline for levelling for the competition should be provided to the competitors.

I propose a "points of difficulty" system. The more points of difficulty, the harder the dance is. For example an Easy Dance should have no more than 9 points of difficulty, while a Mainstream Dance should have no more than 18 points of difficulty, and so on.

Points of difficulty can be attributed to the following dance characteristics:
- Walls – 0 points for 1 wall, 1 point for 2 wall, 2 points for 4 wall
- Turn – 1 point for each ¼ turn in either direction, i.e. 2 points for a ½ turn
- Syncopation – 1 point for each different split beat "1&". Mirror images or repetitions of moves are for free
- Speed – 1 point for each 10bpm over 140 bpm, 1 point for each 10bpm below 100 bpm
- Holds – 1 point for each distinct hold. Mirror images or repetitions of clusters are for free
- Length – 24-32 beats long = 1 point, 33-64 beats long = 3 points, greater than 64 beats long = 5 points
- Interruptions – 1 point for each interruption (3 points for an ABC dance)
- Body Mechanics – 1 point per abrupt change of direction. Mirror images or repetitions are for free

This will give at least a measuring system that cannot be argued with, as it is based on measurable information, rather than personal opinion or taste.

The numbers can obviously be adjusted, it is the concept that I am trying to describe.

There are obviously other characteristics, such as amount of repetition, or variations in timing of the dance that will also affect the difficulty, as well as the type of actions included in the dance, but this guideline should at least help to check if the dance is going to be appropriate.

The resultant marked up judging sheet, including all the points given and deducted, should be given back to the competitors at the end of the competition to enable them to understand the results and to enable them to improve in the future.

Comedic Competitions

These competitions are not meant to be taken seriously as far as winning, or losing is concerned. The point of them is to get people together to bond, and then to have a good time.

Each act is intended to be line dance related, and may be a duo or group, it doesn't matter. It is intended to be funny, though everyone's sense of humour is different. The acts are often inspired by the lyrics of a song, and then things go on from there with costumes and performance aspects. Actual line dance steps or fitting to music is fairly irrelevant.

Judging can be by audience applaud, or a panel of people. They don't have to be dancers, as audience appeal is the main criteria for judging. If there are prizes, or trophies, it can be tricky to arrange as there is an unknown number of winners. Often a perpetual trophy with the group's name and date of winning works well.

It is important to get the acts registered quite some time prior to the event. Have the applications in writing, stating the music being used and a broad theme name. This will allow time to discourage any duplication of ideas, before the acts have been rehearsed. It would be a shame to have two acts that were very similar on the programme. First come, first served on the choice of music.

Here are a set of conditions to give the entrants that could be used to set up a comedic competition:

- It must be a line dance or line dance related
- Any number of dancers can participate
- All participants must stay decently clothed
- Any music can be used, it need not be country music
- There are no age groups or sections
- Judging is on audience appeal, comedy content is encouraged
- There is a 4 minute time limit from first appearance to the audience otherwise the music will be faded by the DJ
- Dance floor size is ... metres by ... metres
- Entrances and exits are available from all four corners
- Audience will be on three sides. The fourth side is the stage.
- Music must be provided to the DJ, 30 minutes prior to the starting time of the act, as the only file on a USB stick, in mp3 format, with the act name clearly marked.
- Props are encouraged, but must be easily moved and cannot be fixed to the floor
- Any props or rubbish left after the act is complete must be removed immediately after the act
- All dancers dance/perform at their own risk

We have found that having two acts in a row, then some social dancing, keeps the audience attentive and appreciative.

FOR THE EVENT DJ

When there are large line dance events, there is usually someone nominated, or hired to be the DJ (Disc Jockey) for the event. This person is responsible for playing the correct music, setting the programme, and often for "counting in" the dancers. They are also responsible for communicating with workshop presenters and playing the music for them. They may also be required to provide the sound equipment and music.

Making a Programme of Social Dances

It is important that the DJ is knowledgeable, or has been informed about the attendees of the event. They are likely to come from multiple different classes, areas or even countries.

If there are no walk throughs, then each dance will take on average about five minutes. If there are walk throughs, then at least eight minutes per dance needs to be allocated.

Programme by Request

Ideally, if the DJ can collate requests from the attendees, then they can put together a programme that represents the dances that are familiar to the attendees of the event.

I find giving each attendee a single form with five lines for them to write their requests on, works well. I generally try to ensure that everyone will get at least one of their requests. Some will get more, depending on whether they choose generally popular dances, or if they choose unusual, "off the wall" dances that most others don't know. Do not allow attendees to have access to extra request sheets, it will skew the system.

There are a few issues that this system creates.

Sometimes people will assume everyone else is going to request the most popular current hot dance, so don't bother to ask for it. If everyone does this, that dance may not get on the programme. The DJ should be aware of this and occasionally insert a DJ's choice dance to "fix" the issue.

Groups of friends will get together and "fix" the requests by all asking for the same thing to get their local dance choreographer some public exposure. The DJ needs to watch this and ensure that the floor remains full as much as possible.

It may be wise to announce the "fixed" dance as a demonstration dance and trim the music after a minute or so. If reception is good, and the dance seems easy, the choreographer could be invited to do a quick walk through, so the rest of the floor can enjoy the experience.

If a large proportion of the requests are unknown to the DJ, then try to plan at least a third of the programme with classic requests to keep a balance. Don't bunch together the unknown dances, as you may be setting it up for the same small group of dancers to dominate the floor.

If you are running the same style programme for multiple sessions, attempt to watch for single requests that recur from session to session. If someone is that persistent, they deserve to be satisfied after about the third session if possible.

Pre-Programmed

Often an event may run on a programme that has been assembled before the event. Sometimes this will be done by the instructor coordinating the event. Other times it will be done by gathering the requests before the event and then collating them.

Keeping the Floor Full

I have a standard rule that, if there are less than six people dancing on the floor for any particular song, then I will fade the song after one minute. It enables the people that know the dance to demonstrate their knowledge, without holding up a room full of other dancers for a long period of time.

I am also careful of songs that go for much longer than four minutes, and occasionally fade them to move on to another request. It is best to warn the dancers that it might happen before the music is started, to reduce the backlash when it happens.

Try to provide a range of difficulty dances, rather than all hard, or all easy. This will only work if you know the dances that are being requested of course. Also try to separate the rhythms of the dances such as waltzes and cha-chas.

Who is not on the floor?

If the DJ is doing their job right, they will be constantly monitoring who is not on the floor. If it is the same people all the time, then the programme needs to be adjusted to accommodate those people.

Find time to find out what their favourite dances are, and try to ensure something is added that they know every once in a while. If they cannot be included, speak to the event organiser about arranging a refund. They are unlikely to accept, but would appreciate the gesture and feel they are being looked after, even if they don't dance much.

Keeping to schedule

No matter how much pre-planning there is, there will always be something that happens that was unexpected. It may be a dance that needs more walk throughs, a birthday in the crowd, or an accident on the floor. Either way the schedule will need adjusting.

I recommend you under announce the dances being done and have some extras prepared in case you have left over time. This is better than cutting dances that have been promised, thereby disappointing people. Running overtime has its own consequences, with additional venue hire, late night noise restrictions, taxis or busses arriving, or cleaning up afterwards.

If the programme is being announced in pieces, then keep track of the time that each piece takes, and plan the last couple of pieces to finish on time.

Split Floors

Often there will be more than one dance to a specific piece of music, occasionally many. Try to group the dancers that are doing the same version together somewhere, such as back, front, middle or corner.

It may be important to specify the choreographer of the dance for each group, as many dances have the same name.

Counting in

When counting in a dance, it is important to be flexible if there is feedback about being in "the wrong spot". Many sheets are open to interpretation, so the local instructors may not have interpreted the sheet the same way as you have. Try to handle the issue professionally without embarrassing the local instructors, and restart it using the "suggested spot" instead. Sometimes there may be people doing the same dance on the floor having started in different spots. Treat this issue like a split floor.

Announcing the Dances

To make the social as efficient as possible, it is important that the attendees know what dances are being presented and in what order. This means less time wasted from people leaving the floor, and the new group assembling on the floor.

If the programme is pre-planned, then it is good to produce a printed programme. If this is the case, it pays to plan some blank slots for last minute additions.

If the programme is not pre-programmed, then I find announcing brackets of about six to eight dances is about right. It allows you to change things around within a half an hour if there are issues of people not dancing, or specific groups dominating the floor.

This announcement can be verbal, but people never listen, and it chews up dance time. It is better to have some sort of visual display of the up-coming dances. The low tech way would be to use a whiteboard (with good contrast bold writing), the high tech would be some sort of video or running light display with text messages.

Creating Atmosphere

I break my socials into three time zones when planning the programme. There are the introduction, core and exit zones. Each one has a different plan for creating atmosphere.

Introduction

People are still arriving, even though line dancers are usually on time, things happen that delay people. During this time it is best to plan mainly classic and easier level dances to get people on the floor quickly and to enable latecomers to blend in with the early birds.

It is wise not to do the latest hottest dances at this time, because the late comers will be annoyed that they have missed their favourite dances and pressure you into playing them again.

Core

During this time you can programme whatever you like, provided you keep the floor as full as possible. Ensure you hold back a few of the most popular classics for the last exit zone.

Exit

The last bracket of dancing should be kept relatively easy. Many people are tired, and keeping enthusiasm can be difficult. Hold back some high popularity, lower degree of difficulty, dances for the end. If you want to go out with a bang, select the best for last. If you want to go out relaxed, save a popular waltz for the last dance.

Other tasks for a DJ

MC Duties

Being the DJ for an event often means being the master of ceremonies (MC) as well. This may involve handling announcements like:

- Housekeeping, such as location of toilets, food and drinks etc.
- Schedule announcements for workshops, meals and breaks
- Merchandising announcements
- Security messages, such as "don't leave your handbags near the door"
- Birthday and special personal event announcements
- Auctioning duties for decorations and excess food sales
- Crowd control issues if a difficult situation arises
- Handling medical emergencies

Workshop Coordination

If it is a workshop event, then the DJ will need to correspond with, manage and coordinate with one or more presenters. It is important that you provide the presenters with good quality working microphones, with charged batteries. Always have spare batteries available. Instruct each presenter in using the microphone, as each microphone is different, and they may not be familiar with your model of equipment.

Clarify the length of time of the workshop with the presenter.

Monitor the workshop, and discretely communicate with the presenter, should you notice any issue developing. Realise that you are facing and watching the audience, whereas the presenter will generally have their back to the audience, so will not have the same level of visibility.

Set up a series of hand or face signals with the presenters to communicate changing of the volume of the music, and voice. You may need to adjust the treble and bass controls depending on the type of voice that the presenter has. Each one will be different. It is your responsibility to make them come across as clear as possible to the audience.

Monitor the time for the workshop, and advise the presenter when they have ten minutes to go, so they can start their wrap up. If there are any potential run over issues, you will need to get advice from the event coordinator as to their policy.

FOR THE LINE DANCE MANAGER

Line dance activities are managed in one of two ways. They are either run for somebody or some organisation, or run by somebody.

The instructor, DJ or Event Coordinator are either:
- Employees – Responsible to or report to some higher manager or organisation, with reduced responsibility or liability
- Entrepreneurs – Not responsible to anyone else and make all the decisions and take all the liabilities

If you are in the situation of starting up a line dance activity, be it a class or event of some sort, then you need to decide how you want the oversight of that activity to happen. I am using these terms employee and entrepreneur loosely, as often there may be very little financial gain involved. However it is important to understand the effects of deciding on a specific management structure.

Employee Run Line Dance Activity's

If you are going to set the activity up as an employee, then your employer may be one of the following:
- Another line dance entrepreneur

- A council, social club, business or community organisation
- An non-profit association or incorporated body

In these circumstances, the future of your activity will be decided on by the results expected by that employer. They can dictate how and when your activity happens, and what happens to the financial returns. In return, they should also take responsibility for the costs and legal issues involved in running the activity.

Sometimes it is beneficial to set up an association to oversee the activity. The existence of this association, will remove some personal liability issues should they arise. An association is run according to a constitution. This constitution explains how the association handles membership, finances and responsibilities. There are usually government rules regarding what must be in the constitution, to protect members from exploitation.

Having an association, shares the responsibilities amongst a group of executives and committee members. It also shares the decision making power and recognition of achievements. Not everyone may agree on the direction of the activity, so the majority will vote and decide these issues.

It is important that there is a contract between the organisation and the employee that clearly states the responsibilities of the employee, and where they go to get clarification, if a situation arises that is not covered by the contract. Ideally this should be in writing, but may be verbal in simple situations. Be aware that a simple situation can become complex very quickly should there be an injury, or theft at the activity.

Knowledge of licensing and insurance requirements, and who is responsible for them is very important in these circumstances.

Entrepreneur Run Line Dance Activities

Being an entrepreneur does not necessarily mean making money. Many people in this situation may be volunteers, or hobbyists. Either way, they decide on how much to charge for their services, and what direction the activity will go in.

The people who run activities in this manner, need to be aware of the following issues:
- Taxation and government oversight on income
- Financial book-keeping and government auditing
- Legal responsibility, licensing and insurance
- Advertising and customer expectations

Many people that run line dance activities in this manner attempt to do so "under the radar". They often do it as a hobby, and don't declare any earnings for fear of affecting their government declared wage or pension. Most governments allow individuals to earn a small amount as a hobby before needing to go through the paperwork of declaring an income.

To keep their costs down, these hobbyist entrepreneurs generally try to stay "under the radar" in other ways too however. They often don't have the necessary licenses or insurance, nor may they have the understanding of the risks that they are placing on their customers or themselves.

Should there be a theft, or an injury while at the line dance function, the manager of the activity could be found personally liable for the theft or injury and be forced to pay costs. If there is legal issues involved, this could be substantial and life changing for the worse.

FOR THE DISTRIBUTORS

Step Sheet Content and Format

The content of online step sheets has been informally standardized for a couple decades. The main information on a step sheet is:

- title
- choreographer name(s)
- difficulty level
- number of counts
- number of walls
- one or more songs to which the dance can be performed

The most common information beyond that is dance rhythm and length of intro. There have been requests to the distributors over the years to include many dozens of other bits of information on all step sheets, but it was found by the distributors that including more information made step sheets too complicated to be useful.

Webmasters who curate large step sheet archives are able to adjust step sheets to match their own preferred template, and do not need any specific formatting on submitted step sheets.

Corrections

One headache for the online dance sheet distributors is the number of mistakes in the sheets being submitted, and therefor the number of corrected sheets that get submitted. The distributors expend a large amount of effort and money providing our resource material, so it is important that we look after them as much as we can.

If a distributor provides a template to show the way they like their sheets displayed, it needs to be followed as much as possible.

Searching

Part of the job of distributing dance sheets requires setting up a search engine to find specific dances. People go looking for dances for many reasons. It is important to make it as easy as possible to find what they are looking for. Important search criteria are:

- Search by Dance Name
- Search by Level
- Search by Dance Length
- Search by Choreographer
- Search by Singer/Artist
- Search by Song Title
- Search by Song Genre

It is also important that the search can be done using key words, rather than having to be able to remember the complete title correctly. Punctuation like apostrophes and abbreviations like '&' can cause dances to not appear on an otherwise valid search.

Website costs

At its peak, Kickit, run by Peter Blaskowski, was serving up more than 2 million step sheets per month, each of which included multiple visits to a huge database. All this processing power and storage costs money, lots of money. These websites are essential to the development of line dancing internationally, and it is in our best interests as dancers and instructors that we support the website providers.

If there is an opportunity to subscribe to the web sites you use frequently, I encourage you to do so, to ensure the best chance for them to continue to exist.

FOR THE SHEET WRITERS

The hardest part of completing a dance is the preparation of the step sheet. Many top Choreographers do not write up their own step sheets, but prefer to leave it to someone more able to present their creative work for others to read. It must be recognised that the step sheet is the only medium that the reader has, in which the entire intentions of the Choreographer must be expressed. This requires typing and presentation skills. The sheet must be accurate, brief, but complete and easy to read.

It is important to remember that an instructor will use a good dance sheet at least twice. They will use it when researching the dance to teach for the first time. This will be a very thorough work out of the sheet. If the dance is a success, then it is likely that, sometime in the future, it will be used again for a review or revision. At that time, any issues with the sheet will have been forgotten, and any traps will be fallen into again. For this reason, it is important that as much information is given on the original sheet, with as high a degree of accuracy as possible. No-one should have to rely on a video of the dance for clarification.

Dance File Format

There are many digital formats that the dance sheets can be produced in. At this point in time it is easier for everyone if they are submitted to the web sites in Microsoft Word format or RTF format rather than in PDF. This allows post processor programs and spelling checkers to handle the layout better and makes it easier for the distributors to massage the format to keep their website looking neat and organised.

Dance Description

The Dance description should mention:
- The number of walls, or the amount of turn per sequence.
- The number of beats in the dance
- The proposed level of the dance
- The approximate date the dance was choreographed
- The choreographers name and contact information
- The music information
- The music count in information
- The starting foot and foot position
- Any other names that the dance is known by

Music Information

Because of the attention placed on phrasing in modern line dancing, it is really important that the correct version of the music is described, so the instructors that want to teach the dance can get it right. Originally specifying the title and artist was sufficient. Nowadays however, with various remixes and digital releases, it is not so easy. The music information should contain: Artist, Title, Length in minutes and seconds, Speed in BPM, and any information about the version such as featured singers or remix artist. Album name will help, but isn't as important, as songs will often end up on various artist compilations or greatest hits releases. Mentioning iTunes, Amazon or other music sources is a waste of time, as each country has its own iTunes or Amazon interface which may not contain the whole library of available music in the choreographer's country.

Make sure that the name of the artist is spelt correctly, and the full song title on the sheet is the same as the music source song title. Give the genre of the music, be it country, pop, Irish etc.

Song Count In

Many choreographers say start on the vocals. This is not very useful unless the instructor has already heard the music. By the time the vocals have started it is too late to get the dancers started. It is more important to describe the lead-in music prior to starting. The more the sheet describes the introduction, the easier it will be for the instructor to get it right. Some lead-ins can be quite complicated such as for example "Baby Likes to Rock It" by The Tractors.

If you listen to the lead-in music carefully, there is likely to be phrasing there. If it is described in beats and measures, it will be much easier to get right for the instructor. Even better, if groups of measures phrase, including that phrasing is even more useful. For example: "33 Beat Intro" is OK, but "1 Beat + 4 Measures + 4 Measures" is more useful.

Often the lead-in music will contain talking, or noises that have no beat structure whatsoever. Even describing this will be of benefit. For Example: "12 Seconds of Noise", or "3 words", or "7 Beats, 3 Second Gap and 2 Measures" would be helpful to the instructor.

Version Number

No matter how hard you try, there are likely to be mistakes in your dance sheet. Especially once you have released the original sheet, it is important that the instructors can tell the difference between an old and an updated sheet. By including a version number on the sheet that is changed when the sheet is updated, that issue is resolved.

It will also be useful should a sheet be revised with new terminology or contact information over time.

Choreographer Contact Information

If an instructor has an issue with the interpretation of a dance sheet, it is important that they can get in touch with the choreographer. At least include an email address and possibly a telephone number (with international dialling prefix). It is also important to include a little about the choreographer, like their name and the city and country they are from. The date of creation of the choreography is also nice to know. Choreographers do move house and even country sometimes, so details like this help instructors in tracking them down if needed.

Signing a dance sheet with "Dancin' David" or some such does not help anyone and doesn't credit the choreographer's effort properly.

Beat Punctuation

When writing up the detailed steps, it is important to indicate the correct timing for each move. I find that adopting timing punctuation throughout the description helps reinforce the timing as well as having the timing in the leading columns.

I use the following punctuation standards:

; – Semicolon indicates the measure boundaries

, – Comma indicates the beat boundaries

/ – Forward Slash indicates the ½ beat boundaries

\ – Back Slash indicates the ¼ beat boundaries

// – Double Forward Slash indicates the ¾ beat boundaries

So a group of five beats of activity would look like:

"Move 1 \ Move 2 / Move 3 // Move 4, Move 5, Move 6, Move 7; Move 8" and would have indicated timing of "1e&a2345"

Whatever punctuation standard you decide on, make sure there is only enough punctuation to separate the moves, and that it corresponds to the timing that is specified separately. Do not use different punctuation to mean the same thing, it only confuses the reader.

Documenting the Timing

There should be a column on the left hand side of the detailed description that documents the timing associated with the relevant details.

Create Dance Progress Reference Points

I also recommend a column on the left that details the beat of the dance that corresponds to the relevant details. I recommend that the beat numbers start at one and carry on till the end of the dance. I do not recommend breaking the counting into chunks.

By continuing the count through the dance, it enables references to actual beats to be made, making documenting any interruptions much easier. Teachers will chose their own chunking based on experience and terminology. They need to know how far through the dance they are.

Documenting the Turning

At the end of each chunk of detailed description it is wise to refer to the progressive wall that is achieved. This may be done by analogue clock references, or wall references. Those references should be one of the following:

- F = Front = 12:00
- FR = Front Right = 1:30
- R = Right = 3:00
- BR = Back Right = 4:30
- B = Back = 6:00
- BL = Back Left = 7:30
- L = Left = 9:00
- FL = Front Left = 10:30

I recommend these references will be in a column of their own on the right hand side of the dance sheet.

Suggesting the Chunking

Ideally the dance should be chunked into manageable pieces. If there are clean cuts in the choreography at eight beat boundaries, then break the dance there. If there is not, then break it wherever seems appropriate for the terminology of the day.

Interruptions

The interruptions should be documented all together and preferably in order of appearance in the dance. This is done in two parts.

Firstly announcing the individual interruptions, such as:
- Restart After Beat 24 of the 7th Sequence
- Do Bridge 1 After the 4th Sequence and Restart
- Do Substitution 2 After Beat 12 of the 8th Sequence

Secondly, describe any additional choreography that is associated with the interruptions, making sure the name of the sections correspond to the name used in the interruption announcement.

Sometimes it is worthwhile repeating some of the choreography leading up to the interruption to take advantage of terminology that will make the purpose of the interruption clearer.

For example: A Rocking Chair is part of the original dance, but only 3 counts of it are being done, followed by a touch to get onto the correct foot. Then doing a Substitution for the whole rocking chair will make it easier to understand for an instructor, rather than just documenting the touch.

It is often a compromise when deciding on adding Interruptions, and how many. Sometimes if you wait, they cancel out and make it unnecessary, or the dance then requires less of them. It means the dance doesn't phrase for a short while, but there are less interruptions for the dancers to endure.

Don't Mix Clusters into Detail Descriptions

Many people try to use shortcuts in their detailed descriptions by using cluster names and then leaving out detail. This is like saying an elephant looks like an elephant. If a person hasn't seen an elephant before and has never heard of one, the description is of no use whatsoever.

You must define all the actions and turns individually in the detail. The head cues are the place for the cluster names. This may be less of an issue into the future once everyone uses standard terms, but for the present please give us as much detail as possible.

Use the Correct Words in the Descriptions

It is critical for the correct capture of the dance to use the correct words for the foot placements and actions. There are subtle but important differences between the meanings of words for line dancing, which are not so precise in everyday speech. Some important examples of these are:

- Forward verses Front – Forward means directly forward, while Front means a crossing action
- Back verses Behind – Back means directly back, while Behind means a crossing action behind
- Stamp verses Stomp – A Stamp has no weight change associated, while a Stomp does have a weight change associated
- Step verses Rock – A Step has a full weight change, a Rock is only a partial weight change
- Touch verses Point (with the Toe) – A Point is done with no bend in the ankle so the foot follows the line of the leg, a Touch does not have that extension so the ankle is bent
- Touch verses Tap (with the Toe) – A Tap is done with a bent knee so that the sole of the foot is nearly vertical to the floor and is done either across or behind the stationary foot, a Touch does not usually have that extended elevation of the heel and can be done anywhere
- Hold verses Continue – When doing an action over a number of beats, such as a Draw or Sweep, it is important to distinguish whether you are wanting the action to commence, continue and complete over those beats, or the action to happen immediately and then hold for a subsequent number of beats. The execution of

these will feel quite different

- Scuff verses Brush (with the foot) – A Scuff is with the heel, a Brush is with the Toe
- Sway verses Bump – A Bump is with the hip, a Sway is with the whole body
- Bump verses Lift (with the hip) – A Bump will change weight to the opposite foot, a Lift will not change the weight
- Skate verses Slide – A Skate is like a slide but is executed in a curved fashion, a Slide travels straight in one direction
- Drag verses Draw (with the foot) – A Drag is with the heel, a Draw is with the toe or flat foot
- Step verses Strut – A step requires a lift of the foot before the foot can be placed somewhere, If the toe is already in place and the weight is being transferred to that place, then it is just a Drop with a weight transfer, otherwise known as a Strut
- Sweep verses Flare – A Sweep travels along the floor in an arc, a Flare is elevated off the floor while travelling a similar arc
- Close and Touch – A Close is a weight transfer, there is no weight transfer with a Touch
- Cross verses Front – A Cross is ambiguous and could be either behind or in front so needs to be clarified, a Front cannot be Behind
- Touch verses Dig (with the heel) – A Dig comes from a bent knee and is a forward and downwards action, a Touch is just a downwards action
- Bend verses Pop (with the knee) – A Pop of the knee requires a weight change, a Bend of the knee does not have a weight change
- Hop verses Leap – A Hop is done with one foot only, A Leap changes from one foot to the other
- Jump verses Leap – A Jump is done with both feet, a Leap is done with one foot only
- Flick verses Kick – A Kick is done with the whole leg, a Flick is done with the leg below the knee while the upper leg stays in place alongside the supporting leg
- Circle verses Turn – A Turn is done immediately, a Circle is a gradual turn over a number of moves
- Unwind verses Turn – An Unwind requires both feet to be on the floor and legs crossed before the unwind commences, a Turn requires the

weight on one foot only

- Unwind verses Wind – Unwind uncrosses the legs, a Wind ends up crossing the legs
- Pre-Turn verses Post-Turn – Is the turn before the weight transfer action commences or after the weight transfer action is complete
- Diagonal verses Turn 1/8 – If you do something to the diagonal there is no turn of the upper body, if you turn an 1/8 to the corner then the subsequent action will not be diagonal it will be forward or back
- Centre verses Close – When you Close, the available foot is brought alongside the supporting foot. When you step Centre, then you step the foot under the centre of gravity of the body. If the feet were apart prior to the action, then this will not be alongside the other foot

Completely Describe the Moves

When describing the moves, it is important to decide what styling or actions that you want included in the dance and what are optional. If you want claps, clicks or arm movements as part of the dance, then write them into the detail. People can always leave them out if they don't want to do them.

If you don't care if an action is there or not, then don't put it in, or just put it in with brackets around it as a comment or suggestion. If you are going to do this, then put these with the action that they are associated with, rather than as an afterthought at the end of the line when it is too late to work out when you wanted them to occur.

Also when describing the moves, include sufficient detail to avoid ambiguity. Mention which hand to slap with, or which fingers you want clicked. If you want both then say both.

Proof Reading the Sheet

The quality of the dance sheet is a reflection of the professionalism of the choreographer. It is important to remove as many of the mistakes in the sheet as possible. Until automatic checkers come on line, this should be a three stage process.

- Get someone other than the writer to proof read the sheet for obvious typographical and spelling mistakes. This includes making sure the header details correspond to the detail steps.
- Get the choreographer to walk through the dance and test it to the music, ensuring the count in is properly documented.
- Give the sheet to a competent dancer, or even better another instructor, who does not know the dance. They can work through the sheet and dance it to the music, noting any issues needing to be fixed.

It is wise to prepare a good quality teach and demonstration video with music, preferably by the choreographer, to be released with the sheet. However it is even better to get the step sheet right and comprehensive in first place. Instructors don't want to plough through heaps of videos when preparing for class each week.

Remember that information shown on a video won't be available in class to refer to six months later when the dance is requested and the memory is foggy. All the information should be on the sheet when it was released.

FOR THE CHOREOGRAPHERS

Being a line dance choreographer is very rewarding. To see your creation appearing on the internet, entertaining people all over the world, is a wonderful feeling.

In the early days when hardly anyone knew anything about choreography, most of the dances had no known choreographer, and they had no phrasing, not standard beat patterns, no terminology or structure. Because it was all very new and exciting, no-one seemed to care. One legged, off phrase, awkward, it didn't matter. We all loved the dances and thrashed them to death over and over again. Things have certainly changed from then.

Line dance choreography has no rhythm limitations or structural requirements. It is judged by the general dancers with their feet and their hearts. When a ballroom dancer dances to a piece of music, they choose a rhythm, such as Cha-Cha, or East Coast Swing and then stick with that rhythm throughout the piece of music. Line dancers can combine movements from many rhythms within the one piece of choreography. A Cha-Cha move, followed by a Swing move, followed by a Rumba move and it can all work.

As long as the steps, turns and timing are all documented properly, the dancers, all over the world, can replicate the experience the choreographer is creating. It is the Choreographers responsibility to ensure that what is put onto paper is what they intended. Finding a good proof reader and document writer is often critical to success.

Collaboration

Sometimes dances are created by more than one person. Sometimes groups of people get together at a workshop weekend or festival and create a dance to celebrate the event. Other times a dance is created by a group as a teaching tool for developing choreographers. Often it is just two or more like-minded choreographers working together to have a bit of fun.

Either way, it is important that the pieces are carefully crafted to fit together. Looking after the "glue" between the chunks is important to ensure the whole creation flows properly.

Choosing a Dance Name

Picking the name for a dance can sometimes be challenging. Many choreographers just chose the name of the song, or the artist singing the song. Others check out the lyrics of the song and pick something that catches their eye. Sometimes if it is a "training dance" they will use the name of the feature movement in the dance title. Whatever name you choose, it is important that it can be found easily in a dance database or name search. If you use strange punctuation or leading words like "the" or "a", then finding the dance at a later date can be difficult amongst all the other dances.

When making a request at a social, the dancers tend to "shorthand" the names of dances, often even giving the name of a song rather than the dance. If the choreographer selects the dance name carefully, this will be less of a challenge to the DJ or instructor trying to satisfy the request.

Many people are in the habit of adding Baby, EZ or AB to a dance name to signify that it is an easier dance. Often this is because there is already another dance of the same name to the same music, and the intention is to enable a split floor.

I don't encourage this, as many of these dances are only easy when compared to the other more difficult dance. They may not be particularly easy when applied to beginner dancers in a class situation. The beginners also get sick of doing dances that are classified as "baby" dances.

Music

Selecting the music for a dance is usually the first decision to be made. There are many factors to consider before deciding if you can choreograph to the tune.

Are the song characteristics useable?

Please choose music that is readily and legally available to the general population. This is certainly easier than it used to be with digital downloads, but some music is still difficult to source and therefore encourages instructors to illegally distribute the music, avoiding supporting the musical artist.

It is important to choose a piece of music that is of an appropriate length for line dancing. If a song is less than two and a half minutes it seems too short. If a song is over four and a half minutes it seems to go on forever. There are often multiple mixes of the more modern songs. Pick one that is in the correct length range if you can, and clearly specify it on your dance sheet.

If the song is a long one, then avoid writing a short dance to it. If a dance goes more than twelve sequences, the dancers will get bored with the choreography. Sometimes this is impossible to avoid, if an easy level dance is being choreographed to go with a harder dance to the same music.

If the music is instrumental (without any vocals), then it will feel like it goes on forever even if it is less than four minutes.

If a song is too long, you can potentially still use it, but suggest a fade spot so people can trim it to a more useable length.

If the song has a false ending, it is worth noting it on the sheet as a teaching hint.

Listen to the Lyrics

It is best to avoid songs with "Smutty" lyrics. Many instructors have people in their classes that are less liberal than others, so using a song with offensive lyrics may limit the dance exposure. You may not listen to the lyrics, but many dancers do, and it does affect their enjoyment of the dance. Sometimes artists will put out a "clean" version of a song for this reason, such as the Zac Brown Band song for the dance "Toes". If so, note it on the dance sheet. Remember everyone has a different opinion of what is offensive, so consider carefully your selection of song. What you think is risqué or funny, others may think is offensive.

Some songs are just very depressing or confronting, and you need to consider this when selecting your music. A beautiful song is "Children" by the Mavericks. Wonderful to dance to, but if you listen to the lyrics they are very confronting, telling a story about child abuse. Not the sort of story you want to have in people's happy classes, as important as the message is.

Analyse the Music Structure

Carefully listen to the phrasing of the music and plan out a structure for the dance. The technique to do this is as follows.

Using a pen and paper, while listening to the song (probably over and over), make marks for each beat of music that you hear. I call this a dash chart. When you hear the end of a measure, leave a little gap. When you hear the end of a lyrical sentence, start a new line. It will look something like this:

- IIII IIII IIII IIII
- IIII IIII IIII IIII
- II
- IIII IIII IIII IIII
- etc

Once you have the dashes, then you listen again for the phrasing of the song. Follow the dashes, and every time you think a chorus starts or finishes, draw a horizontal line under the dashes. It will now look something like this:

- IIII IIII IIII IIII
- IIII IIII IIII IIII
- II
- IIII IIII IIII IIII
- etc

This will help you work out what size the phrases are and what interruptions there are through the whole song. Once you have done this, you might want to locate any feature lyrics or musical features that you want to make use of in your dance and write them against the dash chart. The dash chart example would indicate a 32 count dance, with a 2 beat Bridge after the first sequence.

Once the dash chart is complete, you can decide on the length of the dance you are going to create, and therefor where any interruptions are going to occur and how you are going to handle them.

Features in the Music

Selection of the music is often the start of a new creation. There is usually some feature in the music that will "tell you" to do some particular action. Check that the structure you plan makes the action "Hit the Spot" each time, before locking in the action.

Only include interruptions if absolutely necessary. Most dancers hate interruptions, especially ones that don't seem to make any difference.

Choosing the Moves

Dance Flow

Ideally each move should flow into the subsequent move. Unless the feet come together, most moves will send the body in a particular direction, especially after a turn. If the next move follows that direction, then the choreography will feel smooth. If the feet come together, with a Touch or a Close, then the centre of gravity will be centralised, and a move in any direction will be comfortable. A change of direction of 90 degrees is tolerable; a sudden change to the opposite direction can be quite awkward, unless it is a rocking action.

Sometimes it is worth modifying a standard cluster to make the following cluster more comfortable. For example, "Coaster Step, Scissor" is common but a "Coaster Cross, Scissor" is more comfortable because the cross of the Coaster Cross helps move sideways into the side step of the Scissor.

After a turn has been completed, the momentum of the body after the turn will naturally assist a good sideways action, and will feel uncomfortable into a bad sideways action.

When choreographing a roll or turn, it is important to describe how you want the foot placed and when you want the parts of the turn executed. Some turns are long and smooth, other turns are "spinny" and sudden. Sometimes it is hard to understand what the choreographer actually wants because there is insufficient description on the dance sheet. Be aware that a "turn and step" will have a very different outcome than a "step and turn".

Badly or incorrectly describing a turn can make things very difficult for competition dancers who are supposed to follow the dance sheet accurately, and they will be deducted points for incorrect execution. Think about how you actually physically execute a turn in your dance. For example: "Side & Turn ½, Side" is stressful on the knee as you turn, whereas "Turn ¼ & Forward, Turn ¼ & Side" is more gentle on the joints and flows better.

The join between the start and the end of the dance should also be carefully planned and tested. If there are any interruptions of any type, then how the interruption blends in with the main structure of the dance, both into and out of the interruption, should be planned.

Selecting the Dominant Rhythm

When choosing the timing for the choreography, it is very important to consider the tempo of the music. Each rhythm has an ideal tempo to execute the steps. The further you go in speed from that ideal, either up or down, the less comfortable it will be to correctly execute the actions for that rhythm.

This does not stop you from using the rhythm movements, but it may restrict the number of movements of that rhythm that it is comfortable to use one after the other.

- Standard Rhythm is generally around 140 bpm.
- Mambo Rhythm is generally around 100 bpm
- Cha-Cha Rhythm is generally around 120 bpm
- Nightclub Rhythm is generally around 80 bpm
- Foxtrot Rhythm is generally around 120 bpm
- Rumba Rhythm is generally around 160 bpm
- Latin Rumba Rhythm is generally around 130 bpm due to emphasised styling.
- Lindy Rhythm is generally around 120 bpm
- Waltz Rhythm is generally around 110 bpm
- Viennese Waltz Rhythm is generally around 160 bpm

This may not correspond exactly to the tempos that are regulated in ballroom dancing, but those speeds are standardised for dancing as a couple, whereas line dancers need to keep their individual frame and balance, so may require an adjustment from the ballroom standards.

If a piece of music has a tempo below 60 bpm, or above 190 bpm, it is close to un-danceable, unless there is a secondary beat that is useable for the slow speeds, or lots of holds for the fast speeds.

Standardise the Difficulty

It is not a good idea to put a very difficult cluster into an otherwise simple dance, unless the dance has been deliberately written as an exercise to teach that cluster. If you are going to use difficult steps, don't try to pretend that it is not a difficult dance. Some difficult steps can be made more acceptable however, by doing them at half the speed. A "Vaudeville" is hard, but a "Slow Vaudeville" is not so hard.

In saying that however, if you string a large number of hard clusters together, one after the other, you will exhaust even the most experienced of dancers. They do need a little down time built into their dances. Sometimes this down time can be the introduction of some symmetry. By doing a chunk with one foot, and then with the other, the brain has an opportunity to have a rest. The more symmetry used, the easier the dance will be.

You will increase the difficulty by making it face more walls, have more interruptions, or use more rhythms. You will also increase the difficulty with the more subtle angles and turns that you introduce.

Creating a Hook

Many choreographers like to put a memorable feature in their dance, often referred to as a "Hook". This can be many things from an unexpected timing change, an unusual cluster or move, or just some form of styling. The intent is to make the dance stick in the mind of the dancers so they will recall the dance even after a long time.

If the hook is successful, often it will be copied by other choreographers, and eventually may become a standard part of general line dancing. This sometimes creates trends in line dancing. This happened with Monterey Turns, Coasters and Vaudevilles in the early years.

Filler Steps

Some choreographers get inspired to write a dance, and then they seem to run out of ideas by the time they get near the end. So all they do is finish it off with a few standard patterns. This is really obvious to the experienced dancer. They often appreciate the "down time" that this gives them before relaunching into the complex part of the dance, but it is still evident that the choreographer "under cooked" their creation.

FOR THE CHOREOGRAPHERS

If you need filler steps, consider putting them discretely elsewhere in the dance, rather than gluing them on the end. Use some creativity. In the dances that the dancers really like, every step counts.

Be careful that there are not too many of the same cluster in the dance. It just makes the dance boring, confusing, or both.

Choreography Traps

The human brain loves symmetry. If a piece of choreography goes one way, the brain expects it to repeat the other way. If the sequence uses a common combination of moves, or clusters, this is even more the case.

If you set an expectation with movements such as "Cross, Point, Cross, Point", then making the next movement a cross behind, will cause issues, as there is an expectation to keep crossing in front.

Some choreographers seem to delight in setting an expectation and then modifying the second half to cause the dancer to be deliberately misled. This can be an interesting quirk of the dance, but can also be the downfall of the dance as well. Too many traps annoy people, but an occasional one adds interest and may be considered a hook.

If an interesting trap is used often enough, in enough dances, it may become part of the standard dancing, and sometimes will generate a new piece of terminology, and then stops being a trap.

Some of the more common traps are:

- Not Yet Trap – This occurs if you sandwich a cluster in between two commonly linked clusters. For example: Vine & Touch; Hipbump 4; Vine & Touch. People will frequently forget the Hipbumps.
- Not Symmetrical Trap – A group of clusters repeats, but not quite the same way. For example: Star 3, Touch; Star 3, Close
- Not That Way Trap – A group of clusters travels one way, but doesn't quite travel the other. For example: Forward, Touch, Forward, Touch; Run 3, Touch; Forward, Touch, Back, Touch; Back Run 3, Touch

- Check Trap – A cluster leads your momentum one way, but the next cluster expects it to go the opposite way. For example: Run 2, Coaster Step. This could be considered bad choreography.
- Which One Trap – A group of clusters repeats identically in different parts of the dance without being part of a symmetric chunk. For example: Forward Rock 2, Coaster Step in beats 9-12 of a dance, then again in beats 28-32 of the same dance. If concentration is lost some dancers will forget which one they are up to.
- Rhythm Trap – A cluster is done using one rhythm, then is repeated but with another rhythm. For example: New Yorker Cha; New Yorker (Rumba).
- Not Normal Trap – A common cluster is executed, but not quite the way it is usually done. For example: Monterey 3, Touch, instead of Monterey Turn.

Be Considerate of Dancer Comfort and Well Being

Monitor the Turns

Consider the number of turns in the dance and the direction they turn. If there are too many turns in a row in the same direction, they will cause some dancers to get dizzy. Break up the direction of turns to avoid this.

The more turns you put in a dance, the less people that are able to do the dance. Do you want a lot of people doing your dance, or just a handful of people? Experienced dancers can always add turns as variations if they desire. Inexperienced dancers are less capable of removing the turns that have been choreographed in.

Ideally, you can arrange the turns so that they can be easily removed without affecting the flow of the dance. This can make the dance more appealing to the teachers and students.

Check the Travel

Consider the amount that the dance travels in any one sequence. Also consider the combined effect of two sequences, and if the travel problems compound with the second sequence. It often pays to dance your creation in a close environment rather than a large hall. This will help find travel issues that will occur when many people are dancing together on a crowded floor.

If you are creating a one wall dance, then this is even more important. If the choreography moves forward slightly, then over a few sequences, everyone will be squashed in one direction.

Balance Issues

Monitor the amount of standing on one leg, or the number of times one leg is used compared to the other. Many of the really old dances are very one legged, usually favouring the weight on the left leg. This causes many balance, comfort and even injury issues.

Working to the Diagonals

Many choreographers, instructors and dancers do not understand the subtle difference between turning 1/8 and stepping forward, and stepping to the diagonal without turning. It is all in the shoulder facing direction.

It is important that the choreographer makes it clear what they are wanting the dancers to do, when executing their creation. Do they want the dancers to be facing into the corner to do a forward action, or do they want the dancers to be facing the front but doing the action towards the diagonal corner.

Turning 1/8 and then stepping diagonal is pushing the boundaries of dancer understanding. If this were the case you would be facing into the corner, but stepping directly to the wall. It is unlikely that the dancers would understand the requirements to that level and would assume you have made a mistake in the description.

Walls and Sequences

Most dances start facing the front of the room. On odd occasions a dance will start in another direction, but this is very rare, and would need to be for a good reason. If so, then state the reason on the sheet.

The dance should be described (including facing directions), as it would be taught, from the start of the sequence through to the end. If an introduction or another interruption causes the dance to start facing another direction with the music, this should be described separately, rather than confusing the description of the standard sequence.

Interruptions

Many dancers do not like interruptions of any kind. When creating your dance, think very carefully whether the interruptions you are proposing enhance the dance. Sometimes there seems to be interruptions just for the sake of it.

If you are going to do some interruptions, then you should properly phrase the whole dance, not do some and then not others. Or explain why the decision was made to ignore apparent interruptions. This will save instructors contacting you for clarification.

Sometimes a likely interruption is so close to the end of the music that it is not worth bothering the dances with it. Occasionally however, if there is a regular recognisable pattern of interruptions. In this case, it may be wise to continue the pattern to the end, rather than adding confusion, if it doesn't change the feel of the dance too much.

If you are required to generate additional choreography for an interruption, either:

- Make it very obvious that it is inspired by the associated music OR
- Utilise a piece of choreography already in the dance
- Preferably a piece that starts like the start of the dance (for a Bridge), so anyone forgetting the interruption will already be executing something similar to it without realising it, AND
- Make it blend seamlessly everywhere it is to connect, both before and after the additional choreography in every instance.

Many dances have been deliberately written to ignore the subtle phrasing and to just enjoy the dance. These dances don't need to be corrected, just appreciated. If this is the case, it pays to mention it on the sheet, so you don't get email suggestions for corrections to your dance.

If entering your dance into a Choreography competition however, there seems to be an expectation that the dance should perfectly phrase through the whole piece of music. Just consider the dancers into the future when making your decision to add an interruption.

Set the Correct Level of Your Dance

I have heard choreographers say "I never put the level Advanced on my sheet because no-one will try it". I've also heard others who put the word Beginner on their dances, so more people will look at it. This sort of thinking is why there are so many problems with incorrect levels of dances. Be honest with your assessment of your dance. If you are going to make it hard, then only the high level dancers will try it. That is a decision you make when you create your choreography. Wear it.

What makes a dance Hard or Easy?

There are so many factors that can determine the difficulty of a dance. Music speed, Number of turns, the list goes on and on. Getting it right is really based on experience and clearly decided reference dances to compare to.

Choreographer Competencies

For a person to consider they are a competent choreographer, they need to be able to demonstrate the following skills:
- Is a competent line dancer
- Can demonstrate how to analyse the structure of a song
- Can demonstrate understanding of the rhythm and timing of a song
- Can demonstrate knowledge and understanding of the required interruptions
- Can demonstrate a knowledge of flow and body mechanics
- Can demonstrate an understanding of diagonal descriptions and terminology

- Can demonstrate an understanding of appropriately levelling a dance
- Can demonstrate and understanding of travel, turn and balance limitations
- Can demonstrate an understanding of choreography traps

For a person to be considered a good choreographer they should exhibit the following attributes:
- Sensitive about other dances already choreographed to the same music
- Thorough about proof reading their documentation
- Minimalist in additional choreography associated with interruptions.

What makes a good Dance?

This is the million dollar question. Each dancer will have their own opinion, and they would all be right. Here are some of the qualities that I have gathered from surveying my dancers:
- Music has a good beat
- The dance reflects the mood of the music
- The steps flow from one to the other
- Not too many interruptions

No doubt there are many more.

OUTSTANDING ISSUES IN LINE DANCING

Plagiarism in Line Dancing

Considering the complete lack of control over the line dance choreography market, line dance choreographers have been very professional in this area. Rarely have dances been deliberately attributed to the wrong creator. Some liberties have been taken to "correct" dances when they are considered to be flawed in some way by people, but usually the original creator is still acknowledged.

Occasionally complete sections of an existing dance have been "borrowed", but even this is uncommon. Generally, existing dances provide inspiration for new dances. This creates "trends" in the choreography industry, as a new cluster is explored.

Often a hard dance will inspire a complimentary easy dance to enable a split floor at social events. This is a good thing, and should be encouraged. Some choreographers even write two dances to the same music to take advantage of this need.

Unfortunately many old dancers cannot be attributed to a known choreographer. Therefore it is impossible to determine if the sheet corresponds to the original intent of the dance. In those circumstances where the dance seems to be wrong, some people correct the dance for their own class. The difficulty then arises if those dances then go somewhere else and the same dance is done differently. Often it's better to just not do the dance in the first place.

If you don't like the way a dance has been written, don't take it upon yourself to change it, just don't do the dance. There are thousands more to choose from.

Legacy Line Dances

Whenever new standards are adopted into the future, there will always be historical legacy dances left over, that do not comply with the standards of the day. Hopefully the original choreographers get the opportunity to update their dances, but even now, many of them are no longer with us, and many creations are attributed to "Unknown".

There is an opportunity for a new breed of line dance specialist to "mine" this vast wealth of legacy choreography and bring some of the gems to light.

Getting It Right

In the current environment it is challenging for an instructor or a dancer to be sure they have interpreted a dance the way the original choreographer intended. Unless they have met the choreographer, they cannot be sure that any videos they see of a dance are actually true to what the choreographer intended. If you haven't met the choreographer, how can you be sure it is them in the dance video?

Similarly, as, up till this point, there has been no standard of dance sheet or terminology, even getting an original dance sheet does not guarantee that the choreographer had the skills to translate their creation into text effectively. If there is no version number, how can you tell if you have the latest one?

Modern technology has the ability to make this easier, once standards in dance sheet and terminology are adopted. Automatic choreography checkers and translators, and even automatically generated cartoon dancers are possible instead of human videos.

Dance sheets can go digital and paper copies will be a thing of the past. The future is then rosy for the line dance community.

WHERE TO FROM HERE?

In this book I have attempted to capture what works for me and my organisation over the past quarter century. I have proposed a lot of things that work for us, that are likely to be very different from what others are doing. If this book makes people think about what they are doing, and commences a standardisation process across the world, then I will have achieved my major goal.

If there are a few less variations in terminology or a few more training programmes for new and existing instructors, then we are moving forward.

I would like to see the professionalism of line dancing improve to the point that it is acknowledged as the unique and special dance form that we all know it can be, from the other dance industries. This can only happen if we adopt and use standards that make sense for line dancing and line dancers.

If you are interested in networking with some enthusiastic, educationally inclined instructors and choreographers, then please contact me. I will develop a mailing list or social media connection so we can develop the concepts in this book to the next level.

ACKNOWLEDGEMENTS

I would like to thank first and foremost my wife and business partner Liz for her support, love of dance, strength of character and firmness of convictions that makes this creation a practical capture of what works in a real line dance environment, rather than a theoretical one.

I would also like to thank my team of instructors that have, over the years, suffered though my experimental phases of creating this set of standards. And of course to my dancers that have unwittingly been my guinea pigs over the years.

Thanks to Bill Bader and Johnathon Hardy for their valuable contributions. Thanks to Shirley Stewart, Sandra Kanck, Sue Morrissey, Elise O'Connor and Judy Hoyle for their proof reading. Thanks to Peter Blaskowski from Kickit and George Crutchlow from Copperknob, for their insight into the Distributor side of the line dance community.

www.ingramcontent.com/pod-product-compliance
Lightning Source LLC
Chambersburg PA
CBHW072143030425
24591CB00007B/259